Reasonable Christianity

Reasonable Christianity

John Rendle-Short

EVANGELICAL PRESS

EVANGELICAL PRESS
12 Wooler Street, Darlington, Co. Durham, DL1 1RQ, England

First published in Australia 1990
First Evangelical Press edition 1991

British Library Cataloguing in Publication Data

ISBN 0 85234 289 6

Printed in Great Britain by Courier International.

Contents

Part 4

Preface

This book has been in my thoughts (and partly on paper) for many years. Numerous people, often unknown to themselves, have inspired me to write it. Always at the back of my mind has been the question: 'How to reach the unreachable?' Faces come before me: students, patients, people met on planes or at lectures — these have been the spur driving me to complete the book. I thank them for their insights and questions, and pray that they, and many others like them, will discover the God of Christianity, and place their faith in Jesus Christ as Saviour and Lord.

John Rendle-Short,
Buderim, Queensland,
1991

Introduction

'What, not another introductory book on Christianity! Didn't C. S. Lewis say it all in *Mere Christianity*? Or John Stott in *Basic Christianity*? Or, more recently, Josh McDowell in *More Than a Carpenter*'?

These and other books like them were excellent in their time. In the past I have given away copies to people who wanted to know about the Christian faith. But the situation has changed. The seed is the same and good, but the soil is bad. The district I live in is called Iron Bark country. These magnificent trees grow well, but little else grows. We have spent many dollars planting trees, flowers and vegetables of all types, as the pile of empty pots and punnets testifies. But hardly anything grows, not even grass — just native plants, which spring up unasked. Partly it is from lack of water (we have had a prolonged drought). But there is more to it than that — some basic lack, even, I am tempted to think, an inhibitor in the soil.

And so it is with Christianity in the cultural scene of the Western world in the latter half of the twentieth century. The seed is good. It has been planted well. The authors have pressed the claims of Jesus Christ as the only salvation for the world. But it all has little effect today. Why? There is a lack, even an inhibitor.

When, as a student, I used to talk to fellow students about Christianity, I could assume that their basic viewpoints, their presuppositions, were much the same as mine. They believed there was a God, although perhaps he had started the world off aeons ago and then left it to its own devices. They knew about Jesus Christ, even if they thought of him as a mere man, not the Son of God. They believed in goodness and badness. They used such words as 'honest,' 'decent' and 'gentleman' — even 'patriotic' and 'chastity'. In short, they subscribed to the Judeo-Christian ethic. The queen was still called 'the Defender of the Faith'. In those days the task of the evangelist was to tell men and women about sin and point out the way of salvation by Jesus Christ. It was assumed, correctly, that everyone believed in God, had heard of Jesus and recognized themselves as sinners. But the scene has changed.

I cannot emphasize strongly enough that the whole scenario has altered. It is past, gone, finished, never to return in its old form. To adapt an illustration used by the late Professor Rookmaaker, you want to shoot a rabbit, so you go to the rabbit warren at dusk and sit down opposite the rabbit hole waiting for him to appear. You wait and wait, but in vain. The rabbit doesn't live there any more. So it is with evangelism. We use the old, tried methods, but in vain. The rabbit doesn't live there any more.

What has brought about this change?

Nineteenth-century philosophers taught that God was dead. Scientists said there never had been a God. The 'God hypothesis' was no longer needed. The theory of evolution had proved that all natural phenomena came about by chance. Theologians explained that the Bible was just a collection of old books written within the culture of their time, a quarry from which to hew useful material. It *contained* the Word of God, but was not *itself* the Word of God. All sorts of consequences inevitably followed:

1. Man is an animal.
2. There is no longer any absolute right or wrong, good or evil.
3. There is no such thing as sin.
4. Therefore, there is no need for a Saviour.
5. The name of Jesus Christ becomes just a swear word.

So today, about five generations later, it is becoming a waste of time to preach New Testament Christianity *alone* to modern men and women: they lack all basics for faith.

I used to carry around in my pocket a copy of the New Testament with the Psalms printed at the back. I do so no longer. If

I could find a copy, I would carry one with Genesis and Exodus bound with the New Testament.

'Whatever for?' you ask. Because before you can understand the Christian evangel, the good news of salvation through Jesus Christ, you have to know about God, who he is, and about man, and the origin of good and evil, of joy and suffering, and, supremely, about the origin of death. And this is all explained in the book of Genesis.

Then in Exodus we read how God dealt with man's wickedness, how he chose a special race of people — the Jews — and gave them laws which had to be obeyed strictly on pain of death. What happened when they broke the laws? That is the story of the rest of the Bible. The final answer is given in the New Testament.

Obviously it is no good reading the answer until you have heard the question. Unless you know something about the character of God, who man is (is he just an animal?), and the 'why' of evil and death, the story of a God/man dying on a cross, and coming back to life again is so much ancient folklore.

Before evangelism, there must be pre-evangelism![1] Without this, evangelism is valueless. It is acknowledged today, by even the most ardent supporters of great evangelical campaigns, that the majority of those who 'came forward' to receive Christ already have some sort of church background. They accept that there is a God. They feel a lack of something in their lives, and they hope that Christianity can put this right. After they have been 'born again' they may or may not continue to live as Christ's disciples.

But what about the multitudes who have been brainwashed into complete atheism? How can they learn about Christianity? This book is designed for them.

Christianity is reasonable

By 'reasonable', I mean reasonable in the broad, popular sense of the word. Granted some essential beliefs, Christianity is intensely practical and satisfying to the mind. Everything has its correct place. All the shapes fit into the puzzle. That is not to say, of course, that all is simple. It is not. The wisest mind can never fully comprehend the mystery and grandeur of God's total plan. Yet the most simple and ignorant can understand enough to satisfy himself. But

Christianity is not just a dusty philosophy. It is *true*. It is a total belief system which has reversed the course of history. It has the power to inflame the emotions. It contains an imperative that demands action. It is the blueprint for living.

This book is written for two different groups of persons. Primarily it is addressed to atheists and agnostics, to outline for them the essentials of Christianity. I assume nothing — no belief, except a belief in unbelief; just an open mind. The person of Jesus Christ is not introduced until halfway through the book. The indispensable requisites of the faith must be grasped first.

But a big problem arises: why should atheists and agnostics read a book like this (unless they happen to have an interest in ancient history)? Why should they bother about what they think are myths and legends?

Therefore, the book is also for Christians to read first so that they can understand for themselves 'the reason for the hope that is in them' and then pass it on to their non-Christian friends.

The passage I have just quoted was written by St Peter to new Christians, thinly dispersed all over the then-known world, many of whom were suffering persecution. He wrote, 'Do not be afraid of their threats, nor be troubled. But sanctify the Lord God in your hearts, and always be ready to give a defence to everyone who asks you a reason for the hope that is in you, with meekness and fear.'[2]

Part 1

Prologue: a French lady

'I was desperate. I said to Philippe, "There's only one thing left, we must try religion."' The speaker was a French lady. Without bothering to make a prior appointment, she had just flown six hundred miles to see me. Fortunately I was able to fit her in. I had met her only once before, when she had consulted me about Jean, a one-year-old boy she was hoping to adopt. I had advised against it. The child was extremely difficult. His real mother had given him up for adoption to another woman as she was not able to manage him. But the first adoptive mother had quickly given him back because she had been unable to cope with him either. So the French lady had been the child's third 'mother' in less than a year. Despite my warning, she and her husband were adamant.

Soon after, the family moved to a new town where they knew no one. Most of their neighbours were Turkish, and they made no friends. Her husband was out at work much of the day, and her daughter (her own child) was at primary school. The boy screamed piercingly day and night. She tried to reason with him. Then she started to hit him. She took him to doctors, but all to no avail. He was obviously intelligent and had no apparent illness.

The punishment increased. She took him to a child psychiatrist and told him she was hitting her son constantly. She couldn't help it. She hated him. The psychiatrist said, 'I can place you in a group with other mothers who lose control and chastise their children harder than they should.' She attended the group only once. She told me how repulsive she found it: eight mothers sitting in a circle, drinking tea and discussing in detail how they maltreated their children.

Things got worse. The bruises became more obvious, the screaming more persistent. One day her daughter said to her, 'Mummy, if you don't love Jean, you don't love me.'

That finished it. Sleepless, haggard, at the point of suicide, she cried to her husband, 'We must try religion.'

So the next Sunday the family went to the nearest church. It was impossible to take Jean in, so she and the children waited in the nearby park while Philippe attended church. She told me that for the first time for months the children played happily on the grass. At the end of the service Philippe waited behind and asked the minister if he would visit them. 'Yes, certainly,' he answered. 'What about next Friday?'

'That will be too late,' Philippe replied. So an appointment was made for late Monday evening.

My friend told the minister what had been happening, and about her overwhelming grief and guilt. 'But that's why Jesus died, to take away our guilt,' he replied gently.

She did not stay with me much longer. As she hurried to catch her plane home, I asked why she had travelled so far for such a brief visit. 'Because I knew you would understand,' she said. I did.

As a paediatrician I listen to many young parents. They tell me their problems. They all have them — otherwise they would not have come. Sometimes they are in despair. 'My whole life has been a disaster,' one girl told me. 'I only get along by making myself a robot,' said another.

It is for people with problems, big problems and little problems, that this book has been written. You may be just such a person, at the end of your tether. Or you may not feel any particular need, but for some reason you are reading this book. Perhaps, like the French mother, you feel guilty. Not that you have done anything terribly wrong. You are better than lots of people you can think of. But still your conscience niggles, and sometimes it gets more active and angrily accuses you. We all feel guilty from time to time.

What is the answer to guilt? Psychiatrist Sigmund Freud taught that everyone, universally, has guilt feelings, which he put down to primeval incest taboos. But he denied the entity of true moral guilt.

Christianity, on the other hand, maintains that man has true moral guilt before a righteous God, and that's usually why he feels guilty.[1]

Christianity has the answer to guilt. It is the only satisfactory alternative to Freudianism — in fact to all atheistic 'isms'. We will return to the subject of guilt in more detail in chapter 6.

1.
A supernatural is necessary

'In the beginning there was nothing at all ... Before the Big Bang of creation, there wasn't even empty space — nothing. Space, and time, as well as matter and energy, were created in that "explosion" and there was no "outside" for the exploding Universe to explode into.'

So writes John Gribbin in his book on the origins of man and the universe which he has entitled *Genesis*.[1] He continues, 'The flow of time as we know it also started with the Big Bang, so that it is literally meaningless to ask what happened "before" the Big Bang — perhaps there was no "before".'

He goes on to explain that 'Strictly speaking we can't describe the evolution of our Universe ... from the instance of the Big Bang itself, time zero. But possibly the greatest triumph of scientific thought has been the achievement, over the 1960s and 1970s, of a self-consistent description of everything that happened after the first one hundred-thousandth of a second, right up to the present day some 15,000 million years later!' The exclamation mark is in the original — and well deserved. For if the statement is true, it reveals a fantastic achievement, but if it is wrong, fantastic audacity. You will understand that despite the title of the book, Gribbin writes from the viewpoint of an agnostic evolutionist.

Gribbin writes with perceptive honesty, and I agree with much that he says. Certainly, at time zero there can have been no matter or energy, not even space for the matter to explode into. The clock of time had not yet started to tick.

I also agree with him that the universe must have had a sudden beginning. The only possible alternative is that matter is eternal: that is, that the universe had no beginning; it always existed.

But to return to the more popular 'big bang' theory, where did the essential energy come from? Where did matter come from? How did time start? The atheistic scientist has no idea. For him, there is absolutely nothing from which it could all have originated; materialism is blank at this point. Specifically, he believes there was no supernatural realm from which the universe could be derived. (Note that the very word 'universe' signifies 'unity, oneness'.)[2] So this is where Christianity enters the picture.

Before the beginning

Christianity is founded on the belief that, apart from this universe of matter and time, of energy and space, of things we can touch and see and appreciate with our five senses, there must be another dimension, a realm of the supernatural. Indeed, unless there *is* a supernatural realm, it is very difficult to see how this universe came into existence at all. But, of course, a supernatural realm would have little practical importance for us unless there was some communication between it and our world. It would have no significance, for example, if our world was a closed system, complete in itself. (For simplicity I shall talk of our 'world' rather than our 'universe'.) But Christians believe that the supernatural is of immense importance to this world and to everything on it, including, most importantly, to us human beings; that in fact there *is* a God, and he existed before Gribbin's 'time zero'. Furthermore, they believe that he purposefully created the world. Here Christians again part company with atheists who maintain that the world came into being by chance.

Other people, particularly those with a craving for Eastern religions, yoga, transcendental meditation, and so on, believe in a god — but not the God of the Christians. I remember talking to a young man, and we got on famously. He kept referring to the Lord, but somehow it didn't quite click with me. So I asked him, 'Is your god in you?' 'Oh, yes,' he replied. 'And in me?' 'Yes.' 'And in that tree?' 'Yes.' 'And in that table?' 'Yes, in everything.' He was a pantheist.

Another suggestion, made in all seriousness, is that there is no 'real' supernatural world or God at all. There is only a mythological god (or gods), made to resemble man — a sort of updated version of Jupiter or Thor. Some scientists go even further and suggest that this 'god-belief' comes as the result of a genetic mutation. Once the mutation has occurred in an individual, it follows the ordinary rules of inheritance and is passed down (as a dominant or recessive?) to the offspring, so that they too believe in 'god'.

How can we find out about this supernatural world of which I am speaking? We can't by ourselves; we can only guess its existence. Tribal elders and Western philosophers of all ages and cultures have sat under their banyan trees (real and imaginary) and made up stories about gods and goddesses and how the world came into existence. Down the centuries people have pointed to so-called 'miracles' as evidence of a supernatural. But many of these have turned out to be fakes, or the products of suggestible minds, and this has inevitably made a joke of the 'god' who is supposed to have performed them. (Please note, I am not saying that miracles never happen. On the contrary.)

Another problem is that some natural phenomena such as earthquakes, lightning strikes, floods, etc., used to be called 'acts of God' (even, until quite recently, on insurance policies). But now, people say, we *know* the scientific explanation for these events, and so they have lost their awe. God has been superseded by science.

How, therefore, can we discover whether or not a supernatural dimension exists, and if it does, what it is like? On reflection we find this is impossible, unless, of course, it leaves tell-tale marks. The question is, does the supernatural choose to reveal itself to us? If not, all we can do is to guess, and search fruitlessly.

But the Christian not only believes in a supernatural (God), but also that it (he) has chosen to reveal itself (himself) to mankind. How, and what sort of a supernatural this is we shall discuss later.

2.
An intelligence is necessary for the scientist

In this chapter I hope to show that, whether they recognize it or not, all atheistic scientists have a problem. (So do philosophers, but that's for the next chapter!)

The scientists' difficulty is this: they *need* a supernatural element (a God) to start the world at time zero. Without it there is no answer to the question, where did Matter + Space + Energy + Time come from?

You may say that merely pushes the problem back a stage further. If a God was required to create matter, etc. (and here I am referring specifically to the God of the Hebrews and Christians), then who created God?

Little boys love to ask this question. They think they have caught the teacher out. But it is a non-question. God was not created. By definition he is eternal. He has always existed and always will. He *is*. Further than this we cannot go. We are finite creatures of limited knowledge. It is pointless to ask questions of this sort. We cannot know the answer unless God himself chooses to tell us, which he has not.

Life from non-life

So to the next problem. How did life come from non-life, organic from inorganic?

Until the nineteenth century, scientists believed in 'spontaneous generation'. They could leave meat lying around, and when they came back several weeks later it was full of maggots. Where had these come from? Obviously from the meat. This, they believed, must be because of 'spontaneous generation'. It was not until the 1860s that Louis Pasteur demonstrated experimentally that life could not develop from non-living matter in such circumstances. Spontaneous generation does not occur.[1]

It is reported that in his original demonstration before the Sorbonne in Paris in 1864, Pasteur said, 'And, therefore, gentlemen, I would point to that liquid and say to you, I have taken my drop of water from the immensity of creation, and I have taken it full of the elements fitted for the development of inferior beings. And I wait, I watch, I question it, begging it to recommence for me the beautiful spectacle of the first creation. But it is dumb — dumb ever since these experiments were begun several years ago; it is dumb because I have kept from it the only thing which man cannot produce — from the germs which float in the air — from life, for life is a germ and a germ is life. Never will the doctrine of spontaneous generation recover from the mortal blow of this simple experiment.'

But if this is so, how do evolutionists explain the origin of life on this planet? Here, I am afraid, I must become slightly technical.

The single cell

The simplest forms of living organisms are *prokaryotes* and *eukaryotes*. The latter are single-cell organisms such as amoebae. But even these are already highly complex. For example, they have a nucleus containing chromosomes. They also possess mitochondria which contain enzyme systems responsible for oxygen metabolism, that is oxidation, or 'burning', of food molecules.

Prokaryotes, such as bacteria, are simpler. They do not contain mitochondria or nuclei as such. When considering the origin of life, evolutionists believe it is to prokaryotes that we should be looking.

Prokaryotes and eukaryotes (and all other organisms for that matter) have a fundamental factor in common: they contain genetic material transmitted through DNA and translated by RNA. Hence the comment by a writer, in a scientific journal: 'In the beginning DNA — or perhaps better RNA.'

These simple (only relatively simple, that is) organisms are composed of amino acids and other molecules. Evolutionists believe that millions of years ago the raw material for these amino acids, (H_2, NH_3, CH_4, CO_2, H_20, etc.,) was present in a 'primordial soup'. It is hypothesized that one day some energy source — perhaps a lightning strike — passed through the 'soup' causing the formation of the amino acids essential for life, especially for the bases in DNA — adenine, cytosine, guanine and thymine.

Amino acids have been made in the laboratory

Now it is a fact that this reaction can be, and has been, synthesized in the laboratory. But here a point of significance occurs. In the laboratory all the amino acid molecules so produced are both left-handed (laevorotatory, or L types) and right-handed (dextrorotatory, or D types) in equal parts. But biologically produced amino acid molecules found in living organisms are universally left-handed. The 'handedness' of a simple molecule does not affect its chemical properties, but is of vital importance in its relationship with other asymmetrical molecules with which it has to react. An illustration would be that you can only fit your left foot into a shoe made for the left foot.

How do evolutionists react to this work on the left-handedness of naturally occurring amino acid molecules? At first they are delighted. They point out, quite correctly, that since the molecules of all living beings are universally left-handed, this surely means that they all have some relationship to one another. And so, the evolutionists continue, presumably the amino acids found in living matter originated from a unique, once-only causative event, which happened to be left-handed.

The evolutionists would argue further that this is evidence that all living creatures come from the same remote common ancestor.

But an alternative suggestion, which also accounts for the facts, is that all living things have the same essential design. To illustrate: the modern motor car did not *evolve* from Stephenson's *Rocket*. The point in common between the *Rocket* and all automobiles up to the modern motor car is the *design*, which in almost every case incorporates a powered vehicle travelling on four wheels.

Similarly, the original laboratory amino acid experiment only succeeded because it had been designed and constructed by scientists of brilliant intelligence. The glassware and chemicals didn't one day fly together from all parts of the laboratory and assemble themselves. The electricity had to be connected to the mains. Even if the laboratory had been locked up for a few thousand years to give time for the experiment to commence spontaneously, no amino acids would have eventuated. Why? Because much thought, work and intelligence was required. If these things don't happen by chance today, why were they any more likely to have occurred billions of years ago?

To recapitulate, when an electric current is passed through a 'soup' containing the basic chemicals, equal numbers of L and D amino acids are synthesized, but these are useless to form life. So for the once-only event some other mechanism must have operated. The primordial soup and lightning strike idea, apparently so attractive at first, and so frequently quoted in textbooks, just won't do.

Also, if the reaction occurred only once, it is neither repeatable nor refutable. Thus, it is something which can never be proved or disproved. You either believe it, or you don't. And so immediately it ceases to be a matter of experimental science and enters the realm of metaphysics. Or, since the concept has to be accepted by faith, we would not be far wrong if we called it religious.

Furthermore, even if the once-only event had produced the required forms of amino acids — all left-handed and in the correct proportions — this does not mean life could commence.

A programme

Amino acids are merely the building blocks, not the building. Something further is needed: intelligent information — a blueprint, so that molecules can be arranged in the correct sequence. To change the metaphor, the 'computer' has to be programmed. 'Hardware' without 'software' is useless.

But this 'computer' of living cells is quite unlike any we possess (although scientists are at present working hopefully towards it). It is unique in that it must have the capacity for self-replication. That is, both the 'hardware' and 'software' must be such that they are capable of correcting errors and even designing and building new models. And all this has to happen, not just once, by chance, in the little primordial pond, millions of years ago, but continually, in every living cell, in every living thing, all the time. Here we approach the essential difference between a gram of living cells in one test-tube, and a gram of the component chemical elements (carbon, oxygen, hydrogen, nitrogen, etc.) in a second test-tube. It is the difference between a live sheep and mince on a butcher's slab. The cells of the sheep are living and are capable of replication because they have been 'programmed'. An 'intelligence' has imbued them with life. But mince is dead and doomed to decay.

Sometimes I pull a leaf off an African violet and poke the stem into some moist soil in a pot. Soon the leaf looks tatty and brown. But if I remember to water it, after three to four weeks a miniature green leaf appears above the earth close to the stem, then another, and another. They grow bigger, and after a few months flowers develop, identical to those on the original plant. But if I stuck a knitting needle into the soil instead, what would happen? Nothing (except that my wife would want her needle back!). There is a world of difference between non-living atoms and molecules which can never replicate and grow, and a living organism — the cells in the leaf — which possesses intelligent information, a 'programme'.

I may have given the impression that the origin of life on earth is the only problem for evolutionists. But it is not. As a medical doctor, I am constantly amazed at the complexity and intricacy of function in the human body, made up of millions of living cells.

You can consider any part you like: the working of the eye, or the endocrine system, or the complex biochemistry necessary for the excretion of waste products — I could go on and on. Over the years I have listened to countless lectures by researchers describing their findings. Constantly they say that it was all far more complicated than they had ever anticipated. They grow ecstatic at the wonder of what they have discovered. Yet, they say, there are still many more questions to be answered — and they would like a further research grant to be able to prove their point!

Evolutionists believe that, given the millions of years available (as many as you like), life could have been synthesized by chance without an intelligence, without Pasteur's 'germ'. They hint that, given enough time, the impossible becomes possible, the possible probable, the probable virtually certain. They argue that, according to the probability formula, if Matter (M) is infinity, and Energy (E) is infinity, and Time (t) is infinity, then the probability of an event's occurring is 1. That is

$$M + E + t = \text{Life.}$$

So the seemingly impossible has become virtually certain. And this must truly be so for *irreversible* reactions, such as ordinarily occur in the chemistry laboratory. But biological reactions, working under the influence of DNA (the programme for life), are *reversible*. This is because they work through enzyme systems. And with reversible reactions the law of probability does not hold good.

So the required formula is not just

Matter + Energy + Time = Life

but,

Matter + Energy + Time + *Programme* (DNA) = Life

Origin of the intelligence

But where does this programme or intelligence come from? 'Sperm from outer space,' say Professor Sir Fred Hoyle and Professor Chandra Wickramasinghe.[2] They suggest that sperm containing the first life programme was brought to earth on meteorites millions of years ago. But where did these sperm originate? Hoyle and Wickramasinghe call this the 'monster spectre which keeps beckoning'. They continue, 'Just as the brain of Shakespeare was necessary to produce the famous sonnets, so prior information was required to produce a living cell. But information from where? From some pre-existing life-form, one is tempted to answer.'

Then they quote a story by Tommy Gold: 'A lecturer had spoken about the nature of the earth and the planets. Afterwards an old lady came up to him, claiming to know a superior theory ... "We don't live on a ball revolving around the sun," she said. "We live on a crust of earth on the back of a giant turtle." Astonished, the lecturer asked, "And what does the turtle stand on?" "On the back of a second, still larger turtle," was the confident answer. "But what holds up the second turtle?" persisted the lecturer. "It's no use, mister," the old lady replied. "It's turtles all the way down."'

If Hoyle is asked, 'Do you think that the programme, or intelligence, could be the God of the Bible?' he replies, 'No.' I will explain his reasons later.

Despite what Hoyle says, it is tempting to link the necessary intelligence with the necessary supernatural, and say this is what a Christian means when he talks of God. Certainly the suggestion seems worth exploring further.

The human mind

Evolutionists have yet another problem. Scientists studying the intricacy of nature, and artists admiring its beauty, are overwhelmed. They write of Nature with a capital 'N'. But if nature is so awe-inspiring, what of the human mind which enables us to unravel its secrets? This is such an important subject that we shall return to it also when we discuss the difference between man and animals. As we shall discover, there are fundamental differences between the intelligence of man and even the highest animal. How did this come about? How could some hominid, some *Homo erectus,* evolve into *Homo sapiens* — man the wise — man with overwhelming intelligence? Atheistic evolutionists have no satisfactory answer to this question. On the other hand, theistic evolutionists usually suggest that to make man in his own image, God stamped his own likeness on to one of the many ape-like creatures living at the time. This suggestion, of course, has no basis in Scripture. It is merely an endeavour to reconcile Christianity with a belief in evolution.[3]

Summary

The logical scientist must explain three critical phases in the origin of existence.

1. *The origin of the universe.* If everything goes back to the 'big bang', where did the energy, matter and space come from? What was there before 'time zero'?
2. *The origin of life from inert matter.* Scientific evidence indicates that an intelligence is needed. What is this intelligence? Does it exist elsewhere in the universe? Scientists who explore outer space seem to believe there must be intelligence somewhere 'out there'.
3. *The origin of the human mind.* Why is the human brain so immensely superior to that of animals? It must be far more than the

fact that humans speak and animals don't. But what is the missing factor?

In my reading of evolutionary literature I have not come upon satisfactory answers to these three questions. The possibility that any wonder can occur spontaneously, given aeons of time, just doesn't make sense unless intelligence (programme, e.g. specific sequences or DNA) is added to the formula.

There are many other scientific difficulties to the theory of evolution which are outside the scope of this book. To mention a few: the universal gaps in the fossil record (the so-called 'missing links'); the acknowledged circular reasoning of dating index fossils from the age of the rocks, and rocks from the age of the fossils they contain; the frequent inconsistency of radioactive dating methods; and the incredible complexity of everything in nature. Nothing turns out to be simple although it is often 'beautiful', in the sense that the design is superbly adapted to the purpose.

How could all this have come about by chance? Could there be a designer after all? We will look at this next.

3.
An intelligence is necessary for the philosopher

Over the centuries, philosophers as well as scientists have pondered the existence of God. They ask, 'Can we prove there is a God by human reason alone?' The short answer is, 'No.' Let me explain why, as simply as I can, as one non-philosopher to another.[1]

Briefly, there are two main lines of argument.

1. The ontological argument (Anselm, A.D. 1033-1109)

Anselm, an Italian monk who later became Archbishop of Canterbury, described God as 'that than which no greater can be thought'. He asserted that people everywhere had an idea of a most perfect being.

How did that idea get into their minds? Anselm argued that such an idea would never have arisen unless there *was* such a perfect being. Of course, I have greatly simplified his argument. But I do not need to proceed further, since most modern philosophers have abandoned the notion. They point out, for instance, that definitions do not tell us anything about reality, unless they are confirmed by observation. Merely to define the idea of God is not enough. This does not prove he exists.

2. The teleological argument (Thomas Aquinas, A.D. 1225-1274)

This is more important for our present needs. Teleology is the doctrine or study of ends or final causes, especially those related to evidence for design or purpose in nature, or natural phenomena.

And this obviously links on to the concept of 'intelligence' we were discussing in a previous chapter.

How do philosophers tackle this? Aquinas, an Italian philosopher and Dominican friar, believed it should be possible to prove the existence of God by the study of nature and reason alone without resorting to Christianity.[2]

He believed it was possible to argue, from the natural things we observe, to a great designer or First Cause behind it all. For every event must have a cause or causes. Nothing happens by itself. A tree falls over in a gale. But why that particular tree, and not others nearby? Perhaps because the soil was loosened by all the rain. But why so much rain and wind in just that area? What causes the cycle of weather? And so we could go back and back. Ultimately, if we press far enough, so the argument runs, we must acknowledge some First Cause or great designer of all things. Otherwise they could not have come into existence at all. And this, according to Aquinas, is what we mean when we talk about God.

Design

The argument from design is very persuasive. Do natural phenomena happen by chance, or design? For instance, consider the human eye (an example which haunted Charles Darwin for years). The eye is an extremely complex organ. Light falling on to the lens is directed to the retina at the back of the eye, where it impinges on specially sensitive cells. Nerves from these cells carry the impression of the object under view to the optic cortex at the back of the brain. This is where the actual 'seeing' takes place. Could all this ever have come about by chance alone? According to evolutionary theory all the complex cells which make up the eye are supposed to have developed from more simple cells by advantageous mutations over millions of years.

But how? Of what use is *part* of an eye? Why produce a hole in the front to allow light to pass through if there are no sensitive cells in the back to receive the light and transmit it to the brain? How could the visual nervous system have evolved before there was an eye to provide it with information? The whole complex eye structure, capable of adapting to blinding light or semi-darkness and of viewing the world in glorious colour, able to focus on objects close at hand or far away and to follow a fast-moving object like a tennis ball — how could this have evolved in small segments? Each bit requires the rest to make sense. No one has been able to explain this complexity on the grounds of chance alone. Surely the eye must have been designed.

When philosophers and scientists think like this, they may remember the eighteenth-century English clergyman William Paley (1743-1805) and his argument of the watch. Paley wrote volumes in which he piled up scientific data from nature to prove the creative design of nature's God. In his most famous example he reasoned that, if you find a watch on a remote beach, you know some person must have constructed it. It didn't grow there by itself. In the same way, it can be argued, the intricacy of all natural phenomena — the movement of the stars, the 'laws' of physics, the human mind, the eye, even the structure of a single cell — everything in nature shouts design, and this presupposes a designer.

But there are flaws in this teleological argument. Let me quote Colin Brown: 'If, for the purpose of argument, we grant that there is a first cause, the proof, of itself, does not entitle us to say that he (or it) is the same as the designer ... It is true that the Christian belief in God as the Creator means that he is the ultimate cause and designer of the universe, *but that is an article of faith based on our awareness of God* ... it is not a rational argument to be drawn by those who are capable of following certain arguments' (italics mine).

In other words, we cannot *prove* the existence of the Christian God by arguing from design (which we acknowledge) to a designer (in whom we believe); or indeed by any other philosophical or scientific argument. To say there must be an 'intelligence' behind the universe is one thing. To say, however, convincingly, that of necessity this is the God of Christianity, is quite another. That requires an act of faith.

What does all this mean?

It is impossible for the honest, logical scientist or philosopher who comes to the subject with an unprejudiced mind to conceive of this total universe without there being an intelligence or designer behind it. Perfection in nature is virtually universal. It is impossible to believe it could have occurred by chance. Molecular biologist Michael Denton, in his book *Evolution: A Theory in Crisis* describes the fascinating world of the cell. He writes, 'To grasp the reality of life as it has been revealed by molecular biology, we must magnify a cell a thousand million times until it is twenty kilometres in diameter and resembles a giant airship large enough to cover a great city like London or New York. What we would then see would be an object of unparalleled complexity and adaptive design. On the surface of the cell we would see millions of openings, like the port holes in a vast space ship, opening and closing to allow a continual stream of materials to flow in and out. If we entered one of these openings we would find ourselves in a world of supreme technology and bewildering complexity ... Is it really credible that random processes could have constructed reality, the smallest element of which — a functional protein or gene — is complex beyond our own creative capacities, a reality which is the very antithesis of chance, which excels in every sense anything produced by the intelligence of man?'[3]

But I have to say again: whether or not this intelligence is the God of the Bible, is a matter of faith, *but faith founded on very strong evidence.*

I asked a Czechoslovakian research scientist whether he believed there is a God. He spread his hands expressively. 'Of course', he replied. 'I am a scientist. How can a scientist not believe in God?' But yet, I have friends who can come as far as this, and still not believe in the biblical revelation of Jesus Christ as the Son of God who died for the sins of the world.

4.
The evolution of evolution

Humanism, founded on evolutionary theory, is the dominant belief of the so-called civilized world. So before we look to see what this world is like, socially, morally and politically, we must consider how it got that way.

We have to accept that until the end of the eighteenth century, virtually everyone in the Western world believed in the Judeo-Christian God. That is not to say that they were all active Christians, or that crime, drunkenness and immorality were uncommon. On the contrary, you have only to look at William Hogarth's famous picture of life in the eighteenth century (*Gin Lane* or *Marriage à la Mode,* for example) to see that. But people in Western society did at least acknowledge the existence of a supernatural presence, a deity. They called themselves deists.

Then in the late nineteenth century, philosophers pronounced God dead. But the scientists still needed him.

Blaise Pascal, the famous French mathematician and religious philosopher, wrote, 'I cannot forgive Descartes: in his whole philosophy he would like to do without God; but he could not help allowing him a flick of the finger to set the world in motion; after that he had no more use for him.' Even Darwin, in his autobiography, called himself a 'theist', but confessed that 'With time, this belief has grown weaker.' As we have seen, even a modern writer like Gribbin finds difficulty with the milliseconds immediately before and after time zero. He too needs a God, although he does not admit it.

By the middle of the nineteenth century many people had toyed with evolutionary ideas — Charles Darwin's grandfather Erasmus, for example, and English geologist Sir Charles Lyell and others. But it was Charles Darwin's book, *The Origin of Species by Means of Natural Selection,* first published in 1859, which acted as a sort of seed-crystal to precipitate the super-saturated solution of evolutionary belief nascent in so many minds. As agnostic philosopher T. H. Huxley wrote, 'It is so obvious. Why didn't I think of it myself?'

With the advent of modern evolutionary theory, God was no longer required by scientists. He was not just *dead*, as the philosophers suggested, but he had never existed. The God-hypothesis was no longer required—or so it seemed at the time. But as we have seen, it is not that easy.

Culture and religion

Let us suppose that there really is no God. What follows?

1. In the first place, *man obviously cannot be made in God's image.* So evolutionary theory must be correct in teaching that man is only one of the millions of animals. And, like all animals, he originated by chance mutation and natural selection by 'the Preservation of Favoured Races in the Struggle for Life' (to quote the subtitle of Darwin's *Origin*). Natural selection requires the progressive elimination of weaker, less intelligent creatures, both animals and subhuman. This leads us to the next point.
2. According to Sir Alistair Hardy, in evolution, *death is as 'vital' as birth.* Without it and the consequent continual replacement of the population by new variations for selection to act upon, there could be no progressive change.

Evolutionists believe that man is still evolving by natural selection, both biologically and socially. It is not surprising therefore to find that evolutionary philosophy is basic to such ideologies as Marxism, Nazism, racism, radical feminism, male chauvinism, aggressive capitalism, and other such *isms*. Each believes in the superiority of one group (its own) over all others, which have therefore to be suppressed, or even eliminated. Let me give you an example.

Racism has always been around. But it lacked biological justification until this was supplied by Darwin. In his book *The Descent of Man*, first published in 1871, he wrote, 'The great break in the organic chain between man and his nearest allies, which cannot be bridged over by any extinct or living species [i.e. some missing link], has often been advanced as a grave objection to the belief that man is descended from some lower form; but this objection will not appear of much weight to those who ... believe in the general principle of evolution ... At some future period, not very distant as measured by centuries, the civilized races of man will almost certainly exterminate, and replace the savage races throughout the world. At the same time the anthropomorphous apes [man-like apes] ... will no doubt be exterminated. The break between man and his nearest allies will then be wider, for it will intervene between man in a more civilized state, as we may hope even that of the Caucasian [white man], and some ape as low as a baboon, instead of, as now b*etween the negro or Australian and the gorilla*' [italics mine].[1]

What Darwin is, in effect saying, is that the evolutionary order is Caucasian, gorilla, Negro or Australian [Aboriginal] and baboon. Later in the same volume Darwin contrasts the 'civilized races' with 'man in his wild condition' and 'his nearest allies, the anthropoid apes'.

As Stephen Jay Gould remarks, 'Biological arguments for racism may have been common before 1859 [the date of the publication of *Origin*], but they increased by orders of magnitude following the acceptance of evolutionary theory.'[2]

Darwin's views were used by Hitler as justification for his 'final solution', the extermination of millions of Jews, the mentally retarded, the elderly, and others he regarded as undesirable. In addition he established studs for the procreation of children of pure Aryan blood.

In 1982 two banks in Australia merged to form the National Australia Bank. The first leading article in their *Monthly Summary* was entitled 'Evolution and the Australian economy'. The blurb at the beginning stated: 'It is appropriate that the first leading article of this new bank should deal with dynamic competition ... National Australia Bank is part of an evolutionary process.'

The article commences with the words: 'When Charles Darwin published his *Origin of Species* in 1859 his survival-of-the-fittest concept of biological development would have been familiar to most historians and social commentators of his time. The notion that progress results from violent and cruel strong-eats-weak processes, as described by evolutionists, has never been easy to reconcile with modern philosophies of equity, equality and non-violence. It is little wonder that the subject has sparked such controversy. Governments have long pondered the question of how far society ought to go in support of the weak.

'... The Industrial Revolution of the eighteenth and early nineteenth centuries is commonly cited as a watershed in the development of modern organized business. Yet we look back to that era with some repugnance as we note the long hours, child labour, hard conditions and subsistence wages it produced and the manner in which it dealt with those unable to work through disability or age ... It is impossible to separate the hardship ... associated with the Industrial Revolution from the enormous strides in productivity and living standards which flowed from it ... Ironically ... conditions could only be improved ... as a result of the increased prosperity resulting from a violent survival-of-the-fittest struggle.'

3. *If there is no God, then the Bible can be dismissed as little more than folklore.* You could then laugh at the Ten Commandments, for there is no such thing as the law of God. So human law becomes a social contract — what is best, under the circumstances, for the individual or the state.

History in the twentieth century

Evolutionary philosophy took some time to establish a paramount position. By the early 1920s, although fewer and fewer people believed in God, crime was still mainly petty pilfering (by today's standards), and illicit sex usually meant a one-night stand in a sleazy hotel. This was because the old Victorian morality, founded on Christianity, still persisted. People felt more comfortable that way. But it was as though people were always taking money out of a bank, but never putting anything in.

Decades passed. A new generation, born after the Second World War, was more honest. 'Have it if you can get it,' was their philosophy.

A newspaper strip cartoon puts it this way:

She: 'When you say you can stay here and strike it rich, you're not talking about a legitimate business venture.'

He: 'If it makes a buck for me, I consider it legitimate, lady.'

She: 'And if you fail — if you don't run fast enough, you wind up in jail?'

He: 'That's the risk you take, but it's worth it.'

As time went by, in the absence of God-given absolutes, the law was altered to accommodate new social pressures. A lawyer told me, 'You must remember that the law of the land is public opinion ten years late.' I quoted this in a lecture once. Everyone laughed. 'Yes, it takes at least ten years,' they joked. The public wanted abortion on demand in the 1960s. It was law by the 1970s. Situational ethics had arrived.

Let's follow this through. If there is no God, then man is an animal and there are no absolutes in law, ethics or morality. So what is wrong with sleeping with anyone you want? What's wrong with Peter marrying Philip? Why shouldn't you go nude if you wish? Or, consider the civil law: if you can get away with it, why not sneak fruit off the stall when no one is looking? Don't work harder than you need; the boss makes buckets of money anyway. On a bigger scale, what's wrong with a multi-million dollar (or pound) fraud (unless, of course, you happen to be on the wrong side of the cheque book)? Vicious, violent picketing in a strike is all right if it's for a good cause (yours).

Biological determinism

To whom is modern man accountable if he commits a crime? Many psychologists would tell him he can't help it. His inherited genes and his poverty-stricken environment determine that he should act like that. If his mother was a prostitute and his father a chronic alcoholic who battered him in infancy, what hope has he? Surely no one has the right to punish a man for something he can't help doing? So modern evolutionary psychology has abolished crime. Nothing anyone does is wrong, because there is no absolute standard of right and wrong to measure anything against. Everyone can do whatever they think is best for them.

Other factors

I have tended to pin-point the unfortunate social effects of evolutionism without mentioning the wider aspects of humanism. But please don't think I want to heap all the ills of modern man on to the backs of the scientists of the Darwinian revolution. Let me briefly mention some other important elements contributing to the social mores of twentieth-century man:

1. The Industrial Revolution, resulting in population shift from the country to city slums, with poverty and breakdown in families.
2. The rise of atheistic socialism and Communism.
3. Higher biblical criticism, which eroded belief in the inerrant Scriptures and paved the way for modern religious liberalism.
4. Psychology supplanting religion, especially Freudian psychology with its emphasis on sexual permissiveness.

What comes next?

What is the next stage? For a generation trying to come to grips with AID (Artificial Insemination by Donor), AIDS, the IRA, hashish, cocaine, 'crack' and other hard drugs, nuclear warheads, Satan worship and the New Age philosophy, the world is bewildering. For the old it is the shock of the new that staggers them. But the young accept what they find as the norm. After all, they have never known anything different.

This is the world of today. And if evolutionary theory is true, then all of this is to be expected, and the process of change will continue.

Follow the sequence through:

1. There is no God.
2. So man is only an animal.
3. Consequently, there can be no absolute standard of good and evil, right or wrong.
4. Hate takes the place of love, and destroying lives becomes more common than helping old ladies cross the road. Since death is integral to evolution, it is logical to get rid of the old and infirm. They clutter up the place and consume valuable resources. Hitler with his 'final solution' was right after all. But, of course, his philosophy was founded on evolution.
5. As the memory of the Judeo-Christian ethic fades into oblivion, more laws are founded on the 'will of the people'. Right becomes 'what is good for me' or for the state.

6. If there is no God and no supernatural realm, then there can be no life after death — just a dead end, a hole in the ground, a vase on the mantelpiece, ashes scattered on blue water, bits of flesh picked up after a car-bomb explosion.
7. Some New Age believers embrace death as merely a stage in the evolutionary process: the pantheistic idea of fully expressing the god within.
8. Immortality becomes the transient memory of friends. Or, if you are a scientist, you take comfort in the thought of your immortal genes (blobs of DNA) bequeathed per sexual intercourse to future generations.

I don't believe I am being unduly pessimistic. As I see it, the philosophy of atheistic humanism demands this scenario, and everywhere I go in the world, and everything I read in newspapers and magazines, confirms this prediction. Check it for yourself. What of the future? The outlook is bleak. If this is the world you want, then plunge into it without restraint.

5. Guilt

Freud taught that everyone, without exception, had guilt feelings. He believed these were due to deep-seated incest taboos stemming from our evolutionary past. He acknowledged no cure, no alleviation by psychoanalysis. People had to understand why they felt bad, and get along with it as best they could.

Before we consider what Christianity has to say about this, I want to ask whether it is really true that everyone feels guilt. They certainly did in the days of Freud, but do they today? Do you, for example? I suspect the whole concept of guilt has changed in the second half of the twentieth century. I want to ask, therefore, why some people do *not* feel guilt?

I think the answer lies in the following facts.

1. *Some people lack self-esteem.* In order to feel guilt you must understand yourself to be someone of importance. Otherwise, feeling bad doesn't matter.
2. *Some people think there is no one for whom it is worth feeling guilty.* What does it matter? Who cares? To feel guilty you must have a meaningful relationship with someone. You don't have guilt in a vacuum. Someone must be watching over your shoulder, even if it is only your own conscience. The behaviourist would say you have been conditioned by your upbringing to feel guilt.
3. *Some people think there aren't any rules to be obeyed.* The absolute standards of Western society used to be the moral laws in the Bible, and especially the Ten Commandments. Later, this changed to some sort of 'social contract'. It is as if everyone agreed

it would be better not to steal, otherwise they would never get any work done. They would have to sit at home guarding the TV set in case someone came to steal it. It is just more convenient all round if people agree not to steal.

In Communist countries social moral guilt is induced in a citizen if he contravenes the laws of the state. In China, for instance, to reduce the high population growth, only one child is permitted per couple. Any further pregnancy must be aborted. Great pressure is placed on a girl to agree to this abortion. If she will not submit, she is made to feel guilty before the state, her relations and her friends. They are the moral tribunal. They constitute the moral law.

Who am I? And anyway, who cares?

Many people today are uncertain of their identity. Do you know the story of the man who went to sleep and dreamt he was a butterfly? When he woke he wondered whether he might be a butterfly dreaming he was a man.

The 'man is just an animal' idea has left people endlessly wondering and wandering. They are unable even to form coherent questions, such as, 'What is reality?' and 'Has life a meaning?' And sensible questions are always necessary before we can arrive at reasonable answers.

Modern men and women see themselves as orphans in a vast impersonal universe. No one is interested. No one cares. A writer in a university newspaper expressed it this way: 'I sat all day in the waiting room, but the doctor never came.' Someone else has said, 'The question is not, "Is there life after death?" but, "Is there life *before* death?"'

Do I overstate the case? I assure you I do not. But perhaps people have not talked like this to you. Why should they?

One easy way to take the 'moral temperature' of a society (for want of a better term) is to study its art. The artist — be he novelist, painter, musician, film producer, architect, or whatever — if he is true to himself, reveals his basic beliefs through his chosen medium. To see what I am talking about, visit any art gallery which contains paintings by modern artists, particularly a gallery in a metropolitan centre. Or thumb through the illustrations in *The Shock of the New*; read about the Dada movement; listen to twentieth-century music:

pop, rock, punk or classical. Or read almost any twentieth-century novel: kinky sex, violence and nihilism are introduced as though they were the norm. Perhaps most informative of all, go to the *Theatre of the Absurd*, or, more *avant-garde*, the *Theatre of Cruelty*. (I have to admit I have merely read advertisements for these.)

You may protest that you don't meet this type of thing, that the town in which you live is different, better. You don't see teenagers on the bus or train, 'walkman' plugged in ears, reacting with convulsive jerks in time to inaudible music as though manipulated by invisible strings jiggled by a cosmic puppeteer. The craze for red and green dyed hair with a cockatoo comb may not have reached your location yet. Or perhaps it has come and gone unnoticed. Could it be that you don't see because you don't look? You don't want to see.

I know many people who live blinkered lives. They don't read *TIME* magazine or even the local newspaper. Perhaps you are like that. You have a secure job. You are comfortable. You have a girlfriend or boyfriend. Perhaps you are still a virgin. You have a home. Perhaps you are happily married with a child. You lack nothing. You have no sense of want, certainly no sense of guilt. You know yourself to be clever, successful, witty and virtuous. You have never really done anything wrong. And anyway, if you have, who cares? You are better than ... (pause here to fill in a name). Then think: is this the name of the person you look up to most as the kindest, most honest, most loving? Or is it the name of someone you rather despise? What sort of target have you set yourself? Here is the crux of the matter. Of course you behave better than X, if X is a terrorist or a notorious child-molester, but you well know that the standard you would *like* to surpass is far higher than that.

Guilt[1] is important and necessary

As a paediatrician I frequently see children with behaviour problems. Now, I have heard the phrase (as you may have). 'There is no such thing as difficult children, only difficult parents.' This is certainly not true. Nevertheless, frequently the trouble for the child commenced because of something the parents did or did not do. For example, the mother may be single. Or perhaps the father is an alcoholic and abuses the child. These events put stress on the child and may lead to behaviour problems. Frequently parents tell me they feel guilty for what they have done (more rarely for what they should have done, but have not.) How can I, as a doctor, respond?

I can try the usual patching-up therapy of the behavioural psychiatrist. I explain the principles of child-rearing — the necessity for love, security and discipline, yet progressively this must be loosened to substitute encouragement for the child to exercise self-control and forge his own life-pattern. And frequently this sort of approach is helpful. But it does not get to the root of the problem. Perhaps the mother has never really experienced love herself, so how can she give love to her child? Perhaps her parents never showed love to her, and the child's father only wanted sex, not love (though it was *called* love). Discipline in her life may have been non-existent, or excessively harsh. So she is rebellious and antagonistic to all authority. If I mention God, or the church, 'Church?' she replies, 'You should have seen what Uncle Bill did to me, and he calls himself a church-goer.' Yet she feels guilty because the child's behaviour is so bad. 'Is it all my fault?' she asks. So I try the band-aid treatment. And band-aids have their uses.

But really the problem is that the mother's (or father's) guilt is justified. She (or he) has offended the true moral law of God as laid down in the Bible. That is why she (he) feels guilty. And it will never be put right until she (he) recognizes the fact and comes to God for forgiveness and healing, just as the French lady did.

True moral guilt, so far from being something to be laughed at, or smoothed over, or treated psychoanalytically, is really valuable. Guilt is analogous to the pain in appendicitis. Severe pain, when it is situated in the lower right-hand side of the abdomen, tells the surgeon that there is deep trouble beneath. And when later it moves to the centre of the tummy, peritonitis is setting in. He must act quickly. Guilt, like the pain, is a warning that all is not well.

The greater danger is that so often the parents do not recognize that the fault lies in themselves. Let me illustrate. Australia, like other countries, recognized that it had a growing drug problem. What did the authorities do about it. They launched a $100 million educational programme, complete with a glossy booklet posted to every home in the country. Alternatively, they could have announced harsh punitive measures, including even the death penalty for drug-pushers, as in Malaysia. Will these be of any value? I wonder. Judging by previous educational and punishment measures, such as 'Keep death off the roads' adverts on TV, I suspect they will make little permanent difference. Why am I so pessimistic? Because none of these measures reaches the cause.

Why do people take drugs? Here I am not only talking about heroin, marijuana, LSD and cocaine, but also about alcohol, nicotine, barbiturates and tranquillizers. To the onlooker it seems so crazy. Don't they know LSD blows the brain, or that many world-famous pop-stars and film stars have died of the effects of drug-taking? Don't they know that alcohol is the cause of thousands of deaths and serious injuries on the roads each year, and for the break-up of countless families? Don't they know that smoking causes lung cancer and coronary disease, and that if they continue to smoke they will certainly die from it if they don't die from something else first?

Of course they do! But adverts and scare tactics will never stop drug abuse. Prohibition in the United States turned the nation into a giant game of cops and criminals. The criminals brewed crude, dangerously low-quality alcohol (called 'poteen' in Ireland). Meanwhile the police tried to stop them. Prohibition was abandoned. It didn't work. Even the death penalty for drug-pushers doesn't seem a sufficient deterrent. Why do people take drugs? Here are some suggestions.

1. They are bored, and see no purpose in life. They believe life started by chance, and it will end by chance. This, of course, is pure Darwinism. Evolution teaches that we are chemically determined. 'From chemical reactions you have come, and unto chemicals you will return.'
2. They feel inadequate, and huddle together for comfort. Drugs are a basis for comradeship. Drinking in a hotel restores their confidence.
3. Some find that, under drugs, the world becomes a place of excitement, beauty, joy and peace, which fills a void in their lives. They long to return to it. Others obtain instant mysticism. They believe they see God. But is all this true? A man on a 'trip' believed he had discovered the secret of the universe. But on waking he could not remember what it was. He determined next time to write it down for posterity. One morning, after another successful trip, he looked eagerly at what he had written: the secret of the universe. In scrawly writing were the words, 'The banana is great, but the skin is greater.'

Most young drug-users come from upwardly mobile, middle-class families in fashionable suburbs. The drug problem arises from the availability of lots of money, a hedonistic lifestyle and no beliefs. We are observing the first generation which doesn't believe in anything at all. The generation is nihilistic. They have totally rejected previously held beliefs about religion and morals. Young people are no fools. They judge those who advise them by what they know they really believe. They look to see how their parents (or the media men, or the producers of glossy advertising) really behave. They know that generally the brochures do not reflect what adults practise in their own lives. They listen to their father, beer in hand, lecturing them on the evils of marijuana — and they conclude the whole thing is phoney.

So the solution to the drug problem is quite simple. The parents should maintain a standard of absolute morality, and demonstrate it by their lives to their children. Simple? Well, perhaps not.

True guilt

To return to Freud and guilt, however much people may say they do not feel guilt, I still think Freud was right when he said guilt was universal.

Deep, deep down there is an unrelenting conflict between what a person knows is right and the way he acts. He recognizes that there is a real moral law which he is not obeying, and his conscience accuses him.

According to Freud there is no escape from guilt. All he could suggest was help from a psychiatrist so that the patient could come to terms with his guilt feelings. Obviously, therefore, more psychiatrists and psychologists are required and fewer ministers of religion. According to this view, counselling by a pastor may be positively dangerous. The practical outcome of such a belief has already surfaced in the United States. A minister of religion was taken to court for giving spiritual advice to a member of his congregation. It was claimed he should have referred the client to a psychologist.

Summary

My purpose in the first part of this book has been to establish three facts.

1. That the world is in a mess — politically, socially and morally. I have suggested that the reason for this mess is that men and women

individually have rejected the God in whose image they were created, and have substituted the religion (or metaphysical philosophy, if you think that religion is too heavy a word) of evolutionary theory — a theory that proclaims that man is an animal and can therefore behave as such.

2. If evolutionary theory is true, then it follows that there can be no absolute moral or ethical standards. Even the laws of the land can be manipulated to suit the wishes of the state or individual. In effect, the stronger gains control of the weaker. Thus logically there is no such thing as crime because no one is responsible for his actions. All that a man does has been determined by his genes and environment.

Furthermore, if evolutionary theory is correct, evolution is still proceeding, so this 'world mess' will inevitably get worse, and indeed it is already showing signs of doing so, with the spectre of a nuclear holocaust ahead.

3. You and I, ordinary citizens, are fatally involved in all this. We cannot opt out. It's no use crying, 'Stop the world, I want to get off.' Humanly speaking there is no solution. We are at a dead end.

So much for what I, as a doctor, would call the aetiology, or cause, and the symptomatology of the present mess the world is in.

We have considered this from the human and humanistic point of view. Now I want to start considering the Christian answer.

First, we must have a look at the Bible. Is it reliable? Are the early chapters true history? Or is it all ancient myth and legend? Because if the latter is true, then there is no point in proceeding further. Christianity would turn out to be a gigantic hoax.

Part 2

6.
Are the early chapters of the Bible real history?

This chapter is by way of parenthesis. My book is so much concerned with the Bible that somewhere I needed to give detailed consideration to the foundations on which it rests — the first three chapters of Genesis. I suggest you read these first.

Here I turn to the question of the historicity of the early chapters of Genesis. Is it true space-time history? Or poetry, legend or allegory? The answer is vital to our understanding of the whole Bible, the New Testament as well as the Old.

In Genesis we read that God made man out of the dust of the ground. Man was a new creation. He was not formed from any pre-existing creature.

Some Christians prefer to believe that Adam evolved from a hominid — an animal resembling man — into which God breathed a special type of life to make him into the 'image of God'. They do this to accommodate evolutionary theory. It has no basis in biblical teaching. I suppose you could say that 'God in-breathing a pre-existing dust-returning creature' comes to much the same thing as man being created from the dust of the ground. I certainly believed this myself once. But really there is a world of difference. The change from an ape-like creature to man is too profound physiologically, anatomically and of course spiritually. But let that pass for the moment.

The creation of woman

The creation of Eve poses an even greater difficulty for the Christian evolutionist. See what the Bible says in the second chapter of

Genesis. After God had made Adam he placed him in the garden of perfection (Eden) to till and tend it. But there was a problem: Adam had no adequate companion.[1] God showed him all the animals and told him to name them (which, incidentally, indicates his taxonomic skill, and ability with language. Adam was no bumbling primitive whose tiny head and jutting jaw removed him only a small degree from the apes). I wonder if Adam noted with pleasure the friendliness of the dog and the cat, and the value of the horse for transport.

But none of these answered man's real need for a helper. So God caused a deep sleep to fall on Adam, and then, under that first anaesthetic, he took bone and flesh from man's side, and from them formed woman. God presented her to Adam to be his companion, a 'help meet' for him.

If the Bible is accurate at this point, in the sense that it is true space-time history, then there is no way this account can be made to fit into the evolutionary framework. You have to believe one thing or the other. Either Eve was created from Adam's body — woman from man — or she was just another evolved hominid. You can't mix the two.

Does it matter which you believe? Yes indeed, as we shall see later.

Do you believe the Bible?

Perhaps by this time you are saying to yourself, 'Apparently this fellow believes these things really happened — that Genesis is space-time history, that Adam and Eve were as much real people as Antony and Cleopatra.' Yes, I do. Bear with me a little longer. I have called this book essential, logical, rational, *Reasonable Christianity* for a purpose. I am taking you step by step. Some steps, like the creation of Adam and Eve, you may find hard at present, but they are vital in the unfolding of the total Christian message.

In the Bible, Genesis is presented as history. There is no literary reason to think otherwise. Some new versions of the Bible print poetry as such, in the conventional way — the Psalms are an example. But none does so with Genesis 1-3. Linguistically, these chapters do not have the characteristics of Hebrew poetry.

Could the first part of Genesis be an allegory or parable? A parable is meant to teach a message or lesson. No lesson is drawn by the author from these events. Moses preaches no sermon from them. Chapters 1, 2 and 3, and those following, flow smoothly into the rest of the book. The great detail provided is redundant unless we are reading history.

But the most compelling reason to believe these events really happened is that they are so frequently quoted in the New Testament. For example, Jesus based his condemnation of divorce on Genesis 2:24: 'Have you not read', he asked, 'that he who made them at the beginning "made them male and female", and said, "For this reason a man shall leave his father and mother and be joined to his wife ... "?'[1] St Paul quotes the same passage when he compares the relationship of Christ to the church with that of a husband and wife.[2]

The narrator Luke provides a genealogy of Jesus. He ends it 'Jesus ... son of Joseph ... the son of Enos, the son of Seth, the son of Adam, the son of God.'[3] So according to Scripture, Adam's (man's) only ancestor was God.

There are eight references to Adam and Eve by name in the New Testament, and on many other occasions words from Genesis 1-3 are quoted.

The point I am making is that without doubt the writers of the rest of Scripture regarded the early chapters of Genesis as historical.

The only reason for *not* accepting them as history is because evolutionary theory is destroyed if they are true. But the trouble is, that if you start to pick and choose which bits of Scripture you will accept, and which you will reject, then where do you stop? Do you include the story of Jonah and the big fish? What about Christ feeding 5,000 people from a few small loaves and fishes?[4] Or is this a parable of how we should share our belongings with others? Then we must consider Christ's virgin birth and his resurrection. If all these are myths, the foundations of the New Testament have crumbled away.

Either the first chapters of Genesis are well-authenticated historical fact, as they purport to be, or Christianity is founded on sand.

The rest of Scripture

The Bible can be divided into two very unequal parts.

1. The first three chapters of Genesis tell us of the origin of man and the disaster which occurred as the result of his disobedience. It

explains why there is both good and evil in the world. We discover why man is at odds with, separated from, God.

2. The whole of the rest of the book tells us God's reaction to the events in the first three chapters.

Very briefly, in the latter part of Genesis and the books which follow, we learn that after hundreds of years God chose one man, Abraham, and from him raised up a chosen nation, the Jews.[5] To them he gave the law (summarized in the Ten Commandments).[6]

But time and again the children of Israel (as they are also known) turned their back on God. In order to bring them to himself he often allowed them to be defeated, and even taken captive by their foes. However, he promised that in due time he would send a Deliverer (or Messiah).[7] And at last this Deliverer came in the person of Jesus Christ, son of Adam, son of God. The rest of the story we will consider later.

There is no way in which you can find out about Christianity and its founder, Jesus Christ, except through the Bible. If you have not done so, and are keen to learn more, I suggest you read the story for yourself. A list of important passages is given in Appendix I.

7.
The character of God (1)

We have to accept that we have no way of knowing what really happened in the beginning, nor indeed the ultimate cause and purpose of anything, unless the supernatural, intelligent being whom I am calling God is prepared to reveal it. No one else was there to see. And no experimental evidence now can ever tell us. But, if you are prepared to accept it, God *has* told us about himself in a book, the Bible. So if we want to get any further in our research into the relationship between the supernatural being (God), the universe he has created and human beings as part of that universe, it is to the Bible that we must look. Furthermore, if we wish to discover anything else about God's character and about reasonable Christianity, the Bible must be our textbook.

(The rest of this book will be much more meaningful if you get hold of a Bible and look up the references. I suggest you *do not* use The Living Bible or the Good News Bible, as these are paraphrases rather than translations, and as such are too loose to quote from. Personally I prefer The New King James [Revised Authorized] Version. Many people use the New International Version.)

Absolutes

Whenever we talk about God we have to realize that we are talking in *absolutes*. God is perfect in all his ways, whereas we are not. Everything we human beings know or do is relative. Let me explain. Suppose you hear a pianist play a Beethoven sonata. You are delighted, 'Superb! Perfect!' you may say as you congratulate the artist. But tomorrow someone else comes along who plays even better. And so it goes on.

In this world we can never know absolute perfection. Poets, artists, scientists, judges, politicians strive to do their best according to their own ideas. But always there is some flaw. We have to excuse them. 'After all, he's only human,' we say. But with God it is different. His standard is always perfection: perfect love, absolute justice, complete truth. He is *all* powerful; he possesses *all* knowledge. If you disagree with any of God's works, it is you who are out of tune. His pitch is always perfect. He is right. In fact we can go further: God is his own standard. For example, 'good' is what God says is good. Why? Because God says so. Higher than that you cannot go. Similarly, evil is what he says is evil. We may not agree, but it is not possible to argue with him.

God is the final, infallible arbiter of what is good and evil. So now you know what you are up against. Unless you have encountered the Judeo-Christian God before, you will find this absolute perfection hard to accept.

For simplicity I will describe only a few aspects of God's character. From where do I learn them? From the Bible. There we can learn that: God is holy and righteous; a despot; a sovereign judge; love; a communicator.

God is holy and righteous[1]

To call God 'holy' is to indicate his purity, majesty and glory. The word 'righteous' means to be right or just. It used to be spelt 'rightwiseness', which clearly expresses its meaning. When referring to God the word indicates his truthfulness and faithfulness.

Because God is holy and righteous, he is not indifferent to evil, nor does he regard it lightly. On the contrary, his righteousness demonstrates that quality of holiness which finds expression in the utter condemnation of all evil.

God is a despot

This idea may shock you. But the Greek word *despotes* is used as a description of God in a number of places in the Bible. Usually it is translated as 'Lord' or 'Master'.[2]

A dictionary definition of a despot is a ruler who has 'uncontrolled power' (that is, power uncontrolled by an outside force) and 'absolute ownership'. You probably associate the term 'despot' with 'tyrant' — a powerful, wicked ruler like the Ayatollah Khomeini, who was not subject to any constitutional checks. The fact that most human despots are also tyrants only serves to illustrate the old saying that 'Power corrupts, and absolute power corrupts absolutely.' But God is not human. He is holy and righteous. He is incorruptible. He is a despot (absolute ruler), but no tyrant.

I have highlighted the term 'despot' because I want the stark urgency of the word to strike you right away. If you think the God of Christianity is soft and cuddly, one to whom you can refer when things go wrong, but whom you can ignore the rest of the year without penalty, you are mistaken. Many people create a god of their own imagination. Others worship (or ignore) the one they mistakenly think is the God of the Christians, but in reality he is too small. They compress him into the babe in the mother's arms at Christmas, then put him on a shelf to gather dust for the rest of the year.

But God is all-powerful. He made the universe. Sometimes on a clear Australian night, far from the glow of street lights, I gaze up at the stars. As my eyes become adapted to the dark, I see myriad dots of light stretching across the heavens in the wispy veil of the Milky Way. Other stars are solitary, and occasionally one is so brilliant that I feel I could almost reach up and grasp it. Yet each spot of light represents planets in our solar system, or stars in galaxies stretching millions of miles into space. As I wonder at the vastness of it all, I remember the statement in Genesis that God 'made the stars also'.[3] This appears like a throw-away line. But here we have a point of reference. We humans see the stars as beautiful, intangible, remote. We speak of the immensity of the universe, extending world without end. But to God this is just one small facet of his stupendous creative act.

God made tiny things as well — pigment for orchid petals, strands of DNA. His was the necessary intelligence which created and sustains the life of all his creatures. His intelligence so transcends that of man that it even fashioned the human mind.

We learn from the Bible that creation was by divine fiat (by God's command). God said, 'Let there be light', and light appeared.[4] It was *ex nihilo* (out of nothing). There was not even space before time zero. Look up at the sky. Look at flowers, birds and insects.

Think about your own body. The mechanical perfection of the joints, the complex physics of the eye, the chemistry of digestion, the positive and negative charges across the cell membranes of your brain — enabling you to think, move, remember and reason. How incredibly intricate it all is! Open your eyes to see the beauty of nature and marvel at the greatness of God.

While I have been working on this chapter, three duck eggs hatched out in our duck run. Straight away the ducklings waddled over to the pond to swim — three little yellow powder-puffs bobbing on the water. Who told them it was safe to do so? Not the old hen who incubated the eggs. She is clucking anxiously. If her baby chicks follow the ducklings, they will drown.

Yes, God is all-powerful. 'But,' you may feel like interjecting, 'if he is all-powerful, and loving as well, why is the world full of evil?'

This question has been asked by Darwin, Nobel prize-winner Jacques Monod, cosmologist Sir Fred Hoyle, and many others. Some regard it as a major stumbling-block in their search for Christianity. It is so important we will consider the question in detail in chapter 12.

Absolute ownership

A despot is more than someone with uncontrolled power. He has absolute ownership too. As you consider this you will realize that it must be so. Suppose you make something — anything. Perhaps you paint a picture, or write a poem, or build a shed. Then it belongs to you. The author of a book owns the copyright. The maker of a boat owns it, all of it. This is the rule of our secular world — unless, of course, you are paid to write a book, or to build the house or boat, in which case you get money instead of ownership.

So, if God created the world, it and everything in it belongs to him — totally. This includes you and me.[5]

You may not like that idea. You may rebel. That doesn't really matter. The fact remains, if he is the Creator God, then he is a despot. He has uncontrolled power and absolute ownership over all his creatures.

This is a convenient place to introduce another, more useful title for the Despot God — one which, in an old-fashioned, traditional way, sums up all the aspects of God as despot — we say that God is King or Sovereign. Prior to the rise of parliamentary government, kings were despots, and often not benign despots. Take Henry VIII for example. Feudal monarchs ('my Sovereign Lord the King'), were despots *and* tyrants. Despite this, we are correct in referring to God as Sovereign, since his character is quite different from that of medieval kings.

God the sovereign Judge

If God is all-powerful, it follows that he must either condone evil and be a despot in the popular, tyrannical sense of the world, or he must condemn it. He could not be indifferent and ignore it; unless, of course, he opted out of all concern for the world he has made, as the deists believed in the eighteenth and early nineteenth centuries. But the Bible constantly assures us that this is not so.

Again, being all-powerful, if God does condemn evil, he will do so absolutely. So it will come as no surprise to find that throughout Scripture we read of God's abhorrence of evil and that he is a righteous Judge. We read that he destroys the wicked, and commends those who do good. Abraham recognized this. When he was begging God to spare the wicked city of Sodom, he said, 'Far be it from you to … slay the righteous with the wicked … far be it from you! Shall not the Judge of all the earth do right?'[6]

As I write this I am conscious again that the idea of something being 'absolute' may upset you. In our murky world of half-truths, innuendo and double-talk, nothing is absolute. All is relative. So when we come up against the concept of 'absolute' justice, although in theory we applaud, in practice we hold back. This might go too deep. It could be dangerous.

The 'fear of the Lord'

Considering these two aspects of God's character together — God as despot (with its two components of power and ownership), and God as righteous Judge — it is no wonder that the early Israelites stood in awe of him. Let me describe the scene at Mount Sinai, just before God gave the Ten Commandments to Moses.[7]

The people were told to wash their clothes on two consecutive days, for on the third day the Lord would 'come down in the sight of all the people'. Moses was to set up a boundary around the mountain. He was to tell them to be careful not to go to the mountain or even touch it, for '"Whoever touches the mountain shall surely be put to death. Not a hand shall touch him, but he shall surely be stoned or shot with an arrow; whether man or beast, he shall not live."... Then it came to pass on the third day, in the morning, that there were thunderings and lightnings, and a thick cloud on the mountain; and the sound of the trumpet was very loud, so that all the people who were in the camp trembled.'[8]

What a terrifying episode — ordinary men and women, not particularly good, but not especially bad, facing up before the presence of the all-powerful, all-righteous God, from whom there was no escape! One can sense their terror.

Frequently in the Bible we come across the phrase, 'The fear of the Lord ... ' The word 'fear' in this context means more than to be afraid. It contains the idea of reverence, of God as the controlling motive of life in matters physical, spiritual and moral.

The Judeo-Christian God is no 'tame lion' (to use the phrase of author C. S. Lewis in one of his *Narnia* books). This God is so majestic and 'awe-ful' in the original sense of the word, that I run out of superlatives trying to describe him.

And this is the God who confronted the Israelites in Old Testament times. But more importantly for us, this is the God with whom we are confronted now, and whom one day we shall see face to face. Whether you like it or not, whether you acknowledge it or not, it makes no difference. It is a fact. There is no escape. You are locked in.

I want to discuss two further aspects of God's character: God as communicator and as love. But we cannot understand these until we have considered the difficult subject of God as three persons and yet one — the Trinity. Here, then, is the subject of our next chapter.

8.
Before the beginning

'In the beginning ... nothing,' says Gribbin.
'In the beginning ... hydrogen,' says the astronomer.
'In the beginning ... DNA or RNA,' says the biologist.
'In the beginning ... God,' says the Bible.
Take your pick.

The Trinity

Immediately we consider what happened 'in the beginning' — or even more difficult, what happened 'before the beginning' — we come up against a concept which most people find almost impossible to grasp. I refer to the doctrine of the Trinity — three persons in one God.

Let me introduce it this way. In the first chapter of the Bible we read, 'God *said,* "Let *us* make man in *our* image."'[1] Notice first the word, 'said'. To whom was he speaking? Note also the 'us' and 'our'. Why the plural? Then again, in Genesis 3:22 we read, 'God said, "The man has become like one of *us*"' — plural again. Could this be the so-called royal plural as used by the queen and the pope? There is no reason to suppose so. The only alternative I can think of is that God must be, in some mysterious way, plural. And, in fact, we find this idea common throughout Scripture.

Christians believe in God the Father, Jesus Christ, the Son of God, and God the Holy Spirit — God in three persons.

Each person has a different task or role. Yet it is still true to say that there is only one God. Christians do not worship a pantheon of gods like the ancient Greeks, or modern Hindus. You find this difficult to comprehend? So do I, very. Yet I believe not only that it is true, but that it is *vitally* true. Christianity doesn't make sense without it. I don't think any analogy really helps, but for what it is worth, here is one: water can exist as liquid, vapour or ice. All three are water, yet all are different, and all can be present together in the one system at the same time.

The Trinity in creation

Let us consider the three persons in the context of the creation story.

The Father and the Holy Spirit

In Genesis 1 we read that God created the heavens and the earth. This statement is reiterated in many places in both the Old Testament and the New, although the term 'Father' is not explicitly stated.[2] We also read that the Spirit moved over the waters. In Milton's matchless verse,

> Thou O Spirit ... from the first
> Wast present and with mighty wings outspread
> Dove-like sat'st brooding o'er the vast abyss
> And mad'st it pregnant.

So the first mention of God and of the Holy Spirit, the Third Person in the Trinity, is in the first two verses of the first chapter of the Bible.

Jesus Christ

Turning now to the Second Person, Jesus Christ, naturally we receive most help from the New Testament. St John writes in his Gospel, 'In the beginning was the Word' (Greek *Logos*, which is John's name here for Jesus Christ, as the context makes clear), 'and the Word was with God, and the Word was God ... All things were made by him, and without him was not anything made that was made.'[3]

The author of the letter to the Hebrews makes a similar claim.

He tells us that God, who in times past had spoken by the prophets, has 'in these last days spoken unto us by his Son, whom he [has] appointed heir of all things, by whom also he made the worlds.'[4] And yet another quote, this time from St Paul: 'By him [Jesus] all things were created that are in heaven and that are on earth, visible and invisible ... All things were created through him and for him.'[5]

Do these verses come as a shock to you? Do you understand the immense significance of what is being said? The Bible categorically states that the man Jesus, whose birth we commemorate each Christmas, who was born less than 2,000 years ago, as we testify every time we write the current year (whatever it happens to be), that this man was one of the 'us' referred to in Genesis 1 and 3. As I have been writing this last sentence, I have been trying to see it through the eyes of someone not familiar with the Bible account. The problem comes back to the relationship between the natural and the supernatural. At one end of the spectrum you can probably accept that a man called Jesus lived in Palestine 2,000 or so years ago. At the other end, you can agree that an 'intelligence', whom I have chosen to call God, created the earth. But to say these are one and the same is quite another matter. Personally, I find it overwhelming, but very thrilling.

Let me summarize what the New Testament is saying in these verses and many other places: Jesus Christ is the eternal Son of God. He was and is God, the Creator of the universe.

He refers to himself as 'I AM'[6]— the very name that the Jehovah God of the Old Testament had proclaimed as exclusive for himself. When God spoke to Moses from the burning bush, Moses asked him his name, and God replied, 'I AM WHO I AM'.[7] By this he indicated that he is

1. infinite;
2. self-attesting, with no point of reference outside himself;
3. pre-eminent — before all, and above all;
4. self-existent — he has always been;
5. outside of time — the eternal present tense;
6. unchangeable.

Yet this supreme title, and all that it implies, is also claimed by the man on earth, Jesus Christ.[8] What arrogance — unless of course it happens to be true!

I am stressing this point because many people today deny that Jesus was divine. But Scripture makes it clear that Jesus claimed to be the Son of God in a unique way, and died rather than renounce that title. To the Jews this was the ultimate heresy, and led inevitably to his crucifixion. The Jews threw this gibe at him: 'You, a mere man, dare to claim that you are God!'

Consider it this way. Suppose, in all seriousness, I told you, 'I am God.' What would you think? Obviously that I was mad, 'the type of person who calls himself a poached egg', as C. S. Lewis expressed it. (When I was a medical student I actually met a man who called himself God. He was in a lunatic asylum, of course). Well, then, was Jesus mad in that sense?

Another possibility it that Jesus deliberately set out to mislead his followers. Perhaps he was a rogue, or a mystic, out of touch with reality. Could he have been mentally retarded, conned by his scheming disciples? (Would St Peter fill the bill? But later Peter ran away.)

As you read the Gospels, I think you will find that none of these suggestions really holds water. Mad? A liar? A starry-eyed mystic? Conned? Or truly God? You cannot escape giving your own personal verdict.

We have come to one of the really important crossroads on our search for reasonable Christianity.

Many people can accept Jesus as a great prophet or teacher, even the greatest guru who ever lived. They applaud the Sermon on the Mount.[9] But was he God? No! That's taking it too far. It is at this point that the cults lose touch with biblical Christianity. If you too have difficulty with this concept, I suggest you read one of the Gospels (St Luke for example) and, as you read, ask yourself, 'This man I am reading about, was he a fool or a rogue? Or was he, as he claimed, really the Son of God?' If you study his biography with an unprejudiced mind, I believe God will reveal the truth to you. As you read, sincerely pray, 'O God, if you really exist, please help me to understand what I am reading.'

So in Scripture we find God depicted as the Trinity, three in one: God the Father, Jesus Christ the Son and God the Holy Spirit. You may object to these terms, Father and Son. You may think they are anthropomorphic (that is, they attach a human personality or form to God). And, yes, in some ways that is true. It is a metaphor. But we have to accept metaphors when talking about God. There is no other way to describe him. How otherwise could we mortal, finite beings, visualize the supernatural? Words are not adequate. Besides, the Bible frequently uses metaphors. Jesus himself called God his Father, and God called Jesus his beloved Son.[10]

Summary

In this chapter I have introduced two extremely difficult topics.

1. That the God of Christianity is three persons in one God.
2. That Jesus Christ, the man of Palestine, is also the Creator of the world.

Yet only if these two facts are true is there any hope for you, me and the rest of mankind.[11]

9.
The character of God (2)

In chapter 7 I discussed three aspects of God's character: God as holy and righteous, as a Despot and as a Judge. I left the two other aspects, God as communicator and God as love, until I had introduced the subject of the Trinity. Now, in this chapter, I want to consider the relationship between the three members of the Trinity and how this relationship flows on to us human beings.

God the communicator

We have already seen that God communicates. Ten times in the first chapter of the Bible we read, 'God said ...' To whom was he speaking? It must have been to the other members of the Trinity. There was no one else to talk to. If this is not real communication between 'persons', then the phrase 'God said ...' is meaningless.

On many occasions throughout the Bible we read, 'The Lord said ...' or 'called' or 'spoke' to someone. Sometimes we are told that God 'revealed' himself to a man or woman. We have already noted that Jesus Christ was called 'the Word'. Obviously God has taken great pains to make himself and his works known to mankind. And primarily he has done so through the Scriptures.

The Bible

What an extraordinary book the Bible is! Comprising more than sixty books, it has about forty authors. They wrote over a period of more than 2,000 years. Yet the Bible is a consistent whole, with the same message throughout. It starts at the beginning — or, as we shall see, before the beginning — and takes us through history, past the end of time, for a glimpse into eternity.

The Bible has quite a lot to say about itself, but generally not in so many words. It leaves us to put two and two together.

However, in one place it tells us that 'All Scripture is given by inspiration of God ... '[1] The Greek word used for 'inspiration' does not mean that Scripture was 'breathed into' by God, but that it was 'breathed out' by God — 'God-breathed'. According to B. B. Warfield, a strong opponent of rationalism and anti-supernaturalism, 'What is declared by this fundamental passage is that the Scriptures are a divine product, without any indication of how God operated in producing them. No term could have been chosen, however, which would have more emphatically asserted the divine production of Scripture ... When Paul declares that "all Scripture" is the product of divine breath, he asserts with as much energy as he could employ that Scripture is the product of a specifically divine operation.'[2]

The Bible, then, although it reads like any other book, is in fact unique. It is God's written communication to man. We are even told concerning one part of Scripture, the Ten Commandments, that the original tablets on which they were inscribed were 'written with the finger of God'.[3]

You may think I am placing too much reliance on the Bible. That is not so. There is nowhere else we can go to learn about God. If he is infinite, and we are mere mortals, it is obvious that we can only know as much about him as he cares to reveal. In contemporary literature ('Flavius Josephus' *Antiquities of the Jews,* A.D. 95, for example) we find no more than a few words about Jesus Christ, and some of these are of dubious authenticity.

The significance of God's communication

When I say God communicates with man, do you realize the importance of this? As we have seen, many twentieth-century men and women feel that they are orphans in a vast impersonal universe. But the message of the Bible is sure. We are not cosmic drop-outs. God is there. He has spoken.

At any time you can read what he has to say to you. So you have no excuse for not knowing about God and Jesus Christ.

But further, in order to communicate, not only did God give us his written Word (the Bible), but also he sent his Son, the living Word, the *Logos*, the Word of God. If you want to get a message through to someone you can write a letter, but it is far better if you go and talk to him or her in person. More than that, if you want to show someone something practical, you must go and demonstrate it. Jesus Christ lived on this earth and showed us how to live a perfect life. If you doubt Christ's perfection, get a Bible and read about him in one of the Gospels and see what you think. Even Jesus' enemies could not point a finger at him and say he had done anything wrong. On one occasion he directly asked them, 'Which of you convicts me of sin?'[4] But no one answered.

However, Jesus did not come only to be an example. He was far more than that, as we shall see later.

So, an important part of God's character is that he communicates with man by his *written* Word the Bible, and by his *living* Word, Jesus Christ. God, the infinite one, has intruded into this finite world to reveal his will.

The God of love

Not only was there communication before the beginning of the world, there was also love.'[5] We can read about this in the Gospel according to St John.

When Jesus was praying for his disciples he said, 'Father, I desire that they also whom you gave me may be with me where I am, that they may behold my glory which you have given me; *for you loved me before the foundation of the world.*'[6] And again, 'O Father, glorify me together with yourself, with the glory which I had with you *before the world was.*'[7] These verses tell us that Jesus Christ, the Creator of the universe, had a relationship of love and communication with God the Father before the world was founded — that is, before Gribbin's 'time zero'. And this is the bedrock on which God's plan for the universe, for the world, for mankind, for you and for me, is founded.

'God is love.'[8] 'For God so loved the world that he gave his only begotten Son, that whosoever believes in him should not perish, but have everlasting life.'[9] These and other such passages abound in the Bible.

The original creation was called 'good' by God. Therefore all the goodness, glory, love and communication of God was involved in it. If God says something is good, you can rest assured that it is *very good.*[10] It was beautiful. There was life.

Where God's love is, there can be no hatred. Where there is God's beauty; no ugliness. Where there is God's glory; nothing sordid. Where God gives life, there can be no death. And such was the world as God originally created it.

Summary

I want you to accept three lessons from this chapter.

1. You are not alone in the universe. God cares for you. He has even given us a book so you can read about him for yourself.
2. God is love, and love was the foundation of God's perfect world. So far as we can tell (and here please note that I am only speculating; I cannot read the mind of God) it would seem that God created the world with man on it because he desired a relationship of freely given love with human beings. His whole plan was designed to achieve that love. And he has communicated with men and women about it.
3. God created a perfect world. It must have been perfect because God called it all good.

What about evolution?

Perhaps you want to ask, 'But what about evolution?' Well, what about it? You have come to another parting of the ways. Evolutionary theory says the world was founded on death, 'the preservation of favoured races in the struggle for life', with the inevitable corollary, the elimination of the weak and helpless, brought about by 'natural selection', 'nature red in tooth and claw'. All this is obviously at complete variance with the good world created by a God of love.[11] You have to *believe* evolution as a creed. Or you can *believe* in creation as revealed by God in Genesis and throughout Scripture. Neither can be proved. Either case requires faith.

I am very grateful to scientifically-minded Christians (and non-Christians), for the evidence they have advanced to show that evolutionary theory is full of flaws and that the creation story of Genesis is scientifically plausible. But I am very glad that they have not *proved* (and I think they never will) that creation is right. Because if this were so, it would be possible to believe in God because science had *proved* that he existed. But suppose some experiments later *proved* the opposite, that the previous evidence had a flaw in it. So there was no God after all. What then? No my belief system relies on faith[12]—faith in the Son of God, Jesus Christ, who is the Creator. And this faith is unassailable by the vagaries of scientific theory.

10. Man

We leave our consideration of the character of God and turn to look at man.

Man is an enigma, a paradox: lost and lonely in space, or monarch of all he surveys? He can determine his own fate, and increasingly with his command of nuclear power, that of the world. Yet in Hindu thought he is but a link in an endless chain of reincarnations. Perhaps next time he will return to earth as a toad — or worse.

The common view in modern society is that man is just an animal. And certainly he has much in common with the animal kingdom. He breathes, he eats, he procreates. He has bones, a heart, lungs, blood and an endocrine system — I could go on and on.

Undoubtedly anatomically and physiologically he is an animal. Very importantly, he shares the genetic code with animals. But he is far more than just a human primate, species *Homo sapiens*. Scientists list important differences between *Homo sapiens* and what they would call his 'hominoid' ancestors. Some of these are anatomical. For instance, man is able to walk upright. But most important of all, man has a bigger brain and superior intelligence. He alone can use language. He is able to reason.

The human mind

The human brain — a few grams of mushy material encased in hard bone — has been likened to a computer, but a computer of immense complexity, far exceeding anything man can construct.

Anatomists can dissect the brain and trace the nerve pathways. Physiologists can unravel some of the electro-chemical reactions which take place at cell membrane level. But this is only the machine, the hardware. It is not the mind itself. Something further is required: something which Arthur Koestler called 'the ghost in the machine'.

But does the 'ghost' really exist? Let me quote from a book by C. U. M. Smith entitled *The Brain: Toward an Understanding*.[1] Smith devotes 300 pages to a detailed explanation of the neurophysiological and anatomical intricacies of the brain. He describes the nerve pathways by which we perceive the psychological differences between sleep and consciousness. He describes the modern theories of memory. In the last chapter, 'The Brain and the Mind', he writes, 'The advance of modern neurophysiology has both sharpened the Cartesian[2] dilemma and at the same time tended to obscure it. For few of us realize this scandal in the depth of our culture: this schizophrenia. For, on the one hand we feel bound to assert that minds do in fact act upon bodies, and on the other that they do not so act. On the one hand it is intolerable to assert that the words appearing on this sheet of paper are anything other than the outcome of my conscious intention. I would feel, for example, that it was a total misrepresentation of the fact if one were to allege that they were merely automatic writing ... Yet, on the other hand, it is intolerable to assert that minds do act on bodies. For we have seen in the previous chapters of this book that neurobiologists are well on the way towards a satisfactory physical theory of the living brain. There is just as little room for a strange, immaterial cause like "mind" within the machinery of this liquid state computer as there is within the machinery of the solid state computers used to solve business problems by industrialists.'

Can you sense the tension in this passage? 300 pages devoted to 'a satisfactory physical theory of the living brain'—and it crumbles to dust because the author is honest.

You may be inclined to dispute the difference in intelligence between man and animals. Animals are often described as being 'very intelligent'. But if you study this closely, you will find that the so-called 'intelligence' can usually be explained on the basis of conditioned reflexes or operant conditioning. For example, you can train a dog to fetch a stick, or perform some more complicated task, by rewarding him if he performs correctly, and punishing him if he does not. In a more subtle way, the same method is used to train a child. But the conditioned behaviour of an animal is a far cry from the intelligence of the human mind which can invent a computer.

Some evolutionists regard the mind as the last remaining frontier to be traversed. They believe that, without doubt, one day it will be duplicated by thinking robots, and analysed successfully in terms of chemistry and physics. Recently I watched a BBC television programme on the subject. Some of the experts were quite certain this would be achieved. But who will plan the thinking robot? A very superior human intelligence would be needed to plan and construct it.

However you look at it, man and animals have some likenesses, but even more differences.

I think of it this way: man occupies a halfway position between God and the animals. In the Bible we are told that men and women are made in the image of God. This means that they share some of the attributes of God. I will mention some of these God-like characteristics here, but I have gone into the subject in greater depth in my book *Man: Ape or Image*.[3]

Language

We have already seen that God communicates. He has done so by speech and even writing.[4] Animals do not. Indeed, according to Arthur Koestler, 'The emergence of symbolic language, first spoken, and then written, represents the sharpest break between animals and man.'[5] I am sure you have watched with delighted amazement as a baby learns to talk: 'Mamma, Dadda, Bye-bye, No!' From about one year onwards, more and more words are added to the child's vocabulary. By twenty months the child is putting two or three words together. Grammar is developing. The intricacy of language acquisition is illustrated by the story of a small girl from a doctor's home playing with building blocks. 'Are you going to make a tower or a bridge?' she was asked. 'Make an appointment,' she replied.

Soon the child can talk fluently, perhaps in two languages almost at the same time, yet still keeping them separate. (They often have difficulty with three.) How is this done? How does the human infant learn to talk? No one knows. Linguists say that speech is 'innate'—the child learns to talk because he or she is human. Yet one of the ways we recognize 'humanness' is by the fact that the individual can speak! So this is arguing in a circle. But I can suggest another reason why an infant learns to talk. It is because he or she is made in the image of God, and God uses language. By speaking, the child demonstrates one of the attributes of God.

Creativity

In the British Museum (Natural History) in London is a display on 'The Origin of Man'. Four reasons are given for the difference between *Homo sapiens* and his ancestors, which the scientists believe to be some type of ape-like creature. These are: man has a bigger brain, he walks upright, he makes fire and he uses tools to make tools. A fascinating film is projected of a finch using a thorn to poke insects out of a rotten log. The clever finch is using a tool. But only man can *use* a tool to *make* a tool, and this he can do because he has the ability to reason and create.

But I do not need to tell you that man can do far more than that. Compare the most beautiful of bird songs with a Beethoven symphony; or the elegant but repetitive mating dance of the bird of paradise with a human ballet production, and you will see what I mean. The bird's best efforts are always the same. You can recognize the kookaburra by his inimitable laugh even when he is a quarter of a mile away. Certain birds make certain sounds; spiders build a unique but constant web; animals have stereotyped habits — they seldom vary. But man has original ideas, he can create new things, and does so constantly. In his own small way he mimics God the Creator.

Immortality

From ancient times man has believed his body to be immortal: that after death it passes into another existence not dissimilar to this. So ancient Egyptians provided pots of food and tools for the dead Pharaoh. Sometimes they slaughtered slaves or a wife for use in the nether world. Modern man (like the animals) shows no such behaviour. Why should he? He does not believe in a supernatural existence — for him science has proved there is no life after death. This accounts, in part, for the tenacity with which many people cling to life. It is the reasoning behind the cult of snap-freezing bodies at death in the hope of preserving them until such time as science acquires the skill to bring them back to life again. For many people the only immortality they can hope for is via genes passed to their offspring and on to each succeeding generation. This provides a vicarious immortality, which is better than nothing.

The Christian believes that not only the soul, but the body too, in recognizable form, will be resurrected. The forerunner of this resurrection miracle appeared on the first Easter morning.

Love and altruism verses hate and selfishness

Here man differs notably from animals. But this is a topic of such importance that we will return to it later in a separate chapter.

Man in the image of God

The Bible has no problem with the position of man in the hierarchy of nature. We are told in the first chapter of the Bible that man and woman were made in the image of God. What is the significance of this? It means that man is vicegerent[6] (ruler under God) of the world. Scripture indicates that the main reason for the creation of the earth was as a place for man to dwell (see, for example, Psalm 8). So man has eternal significance. He is a person of note.

I can't make the humanists out. On the one hand they say man is just an animal, a machine. Yet on the other they puff him up to have complete autonomy. The *Humanist Manifesto* puts it this way: 'We find insufficient evidence for belief in the existence of a supernatural. It is meaningless or irrelevant to the survival and fulfilment of the human race. As nontheists we begin with humans, not God; nature, not deity ... We can discover no divine purpose or providence for the human species. Humans are responsible for what they are or will become. No deity will save us; we must save ourselves.' Brave, brave, tragic words.

Summary

The Bible indicates that men and women are important to God. In return they are responsible to him for their actions. You are not a wisp of cosmic dust floating in the void, but a person created to be like God, with a purpose that he will reveal to you if you first come into a right relationship with him. The psalmist asked God,

'What is man that you are mindful of him,
And the son of man that you visit him?
For you have made him a little lower than the angels,
And you have crowned him with glory and honour.'[7]

But I am sure you will agree that 'crowned with glory and honour' and 'only a little lower than the angels' is scarcely an accurate description of most modern men and women. What has happened? There *are* some people to whom these words might perhaps apply, but not to the majority. Why is the world so contrary? Why, ultimately, is there both evil *and* good? We will consider this in the next chapter.

Part 3

11.
The problem of good and evil

'How can Nature be so beautiful and yet so cruel, so wasteful and futile?' asks C. S. Lewis in his autobiography *Surprised by Joy*. He tells us that before he became a Christian, 'I chewed endlessly over this problem.' Many people would echo his words. They have a keen appreciation of natural beauty — birdsongs, flowers, a breathtaking view over a lake or mountain. But what about the destructive power of an earthquake, or the reckless suicide of hundreds of whales beached on the shores of Australia and other places? Laboriously they are towed out to sea, but swiftly they swim back to destruction.

Notice, the question is not 'Why is there good *or* evil in the world?' but 'Why is there *both* good *and* evil?'

For simplicity we will leave the problems of nature to consider only human beings. Think of the happiness of a courting couple or a mother playing with her baby. Then consider war. A fighter-bomber streaks overhead — a machine costing millions of dollars, a weapon of immense complexity designed for one purpose only, to kill and maim the maximum number of people at minimum inconvenience to the pilot.

Evolutionists have no difficulty in accounting for cruelty and waste. It is built into the system. Natural selection requires the birth of huge numbers of creatures, most of which are destroyed so that the fancied few can be selected and the evolutionary process advanced. The problem for evolutionary theory is, how did goodness, love and altruism (the opposite of selfishness) arise? In his book *The Selfish Gene*, Richard Dawkins writers, 'Much as we may wish to believe otherwise, universal love and the welfare of the species as a whole are concepts which simply do not make evolutionary sense.'[1]

While for the evolutionist the question is, 'How did *good* enter the world?' for the Christian the question is reversed. Christians ask, 'What about evil?' God, we read, created the world good. God's character is said to be love, so how did hatred and cruelty come about? Here I must introduce that sinister character, the devil.[2]

The talking serpent

In Genesis chapter 3 we meet a most extraordinary creature, a speaking snake, or serpent. You have possibly seen representations of this scene in medieval paintings. The Bible tells us that the serpent was more subtle than any other creature the Lord had made. But you remember we decided previously that animals don't talk. Yet this one did. Did it really talk? I have to say yes, for as we read on, we find this was no ordinary snake.

It becomes apparent that the animal had been taken over by a higher power, and that power was certainly not God. So there must be two supernatural agencies at work in the world: God and his angels, and the devil (Satan) and his demons.

If you are a materialist who believes nothing exists apart from what can be sensed by touch, sight, hearing, smell and taste, then you will not believe in the devil any more than you believe in God. And there are millions of people in the Western world who would agree with you. But most people in Eastern countries or in animistic cultures are certain there are evil spirits, and so are an increasing number in the West.

The devil today

There are two equal and opposite errors in our view of the devil. We can laugh at, or ignore, the whole concept or treat it as just a useful swear-word. At the other end of the spectrum are those who are excessively concerned. We must remember that the devil's weapons are lies (the opposite of truth), hatred (the opposite of love), and fear (the opposite of peace).

Because the devil — assuming he exists — is second only in

power to God (Jesus called him 'the ruler of this world' and St Paul called him 'the prince of the power of the air'[3]), then his influence affects everyone — past, present and future; of all countries, cultures and religions, including even devout Christians.

What do we know about the devil? Is he just an anthropomorphic representation of evil, that is, is he evil dressed up to look like a person? In Scripture the words 'devil' or 'Satan' appear more than 150 times, and consistently the devil is referred to as 'he', never as 'it'. There is no doubt that the biblical authors regarded the devil as real. If there is a real supernatural world, and if there is a real God, then it makes sense for there to be a real devil too. Certainly Jesus taught so.

We know little of where the devil came from. We gain a hint from Scripture that he was one of the created angels, probably the highest angel. Because of his splendour and beauty he became proud and tried to make himself like the Most High. His desire was, and ever has been, to supplant God as ruler of this world. This he does mainly by attacking God's people.

Scripture tells us that the earth is a battleground between the forces of good and evil.[4] But, unlike the Babylonian or Greek myths, where the gods and goddesses are in the likeness of men and women with human lusts and foibles, the God of the Christian has absolute power and absolute goodness. But opposing him is the devil.

To go back to the story of the talking snake, evil entered God's good world through the devil, working through his temporary instrument, the serpent. Yet both the devil and the serpent were created by God. God made them. So it seems that God must have permitted evil to enter his world of perfection. Why? We do not know. But it must have been for his own good purpose, for God is always in control. So why did it happen? I don't know. Here we have to tread very warily, and not go beyond what God has certainly revealed.

The origin of evil

Some people say, 'Either God created evil in the form of Satan, and therefore God is the author of evil as well as good, or he created Satan as a good angel who later sinned. Therefore,' they continue, 'God is either not competent or not sovereign. In any case, he has demonstrated that he is not in total control of the universe.' What then is?

To many scientists the conflict of good and evil is a major problem. I heard Sir Fred Hoyle, the astronomer, say on British television that he believed in an intelligence which had brought life to earth (via sperm on meteorites). But he did not see how the intelligence could be all-powerful, because such an intelligence 'would have to be rather peculiar to create a world with such horrible aspects as we find in this world'. He pointed out that this had been a problem for Darwin too. Indeed, Darwin in his autobiography tells us that it revolted him to believe that an all-powerful God, who possesses all knowledge, would create the universe by a method which required the suffering of millions of creatures throughout almost endless time. This is one of the main reasons why both Hoyle and Darwin have rejected the idea of God.

So let us collect some facts from Scripture. I have already described the character of God, that he is holy, good and perfect, a God of love. What does the Bible tell us about the devil?

The devil's character

We read in the book of Revelation about 'that serpent of old, called the devil and Satan, who deceives the whole world ... the accuser of our brethren, who accused them before our God day and night'.[5] In the Garden of Eden he seduced Adam and Eve from their allegiance to God in order to deprive God of his due honour, and so plunged mankind headlong into destruction. And this has been his objective ever since.

Christ says the devil 'abides not in the truth'. 'Whenever he speaks a lie, he speaks from his own nature; for he is a liar, and the father of lies.'[6]

John Calvin, the famous French theologian and religious reformer (1509-64), wrote of the devil: 'Truth he assails with lies, light he obscures with darkness. The minds of men he involves in error; he stirs up hatred, inflames strife and war, and all in order that he may overthrow the kingdom of God, and drown men in eternal perdition with himself.'[7]

If Satan is the author of lies, then we must be wary of anything he or his followers say, particularly when they are speaking of such vital concerns as the character of God or the origin of the world. By Satan's 'followers' I am not here thinking of active Satanists. The Bible is quite explicit that the 'whole world' — that is everyone with the exception of true Christians, those 'born of God' — is under the sway of the 'wicked one', Satan (read 1 John 5:18-19).

On the other hand, I don't want to give the impression that all evolutionary scientists are rogues and liars. I have too many friends who are scientists to believe that. Still, unfortunately, a few scientists are frauds. Do you remember the Piltdown hoax? In East Sussex, in the south of England, remains of a human skull and ape-like lower jaw were discovered in 1912. They were claimed as evidence for evolution. But by 1953 scientific facts had proved them to have been assembled as a hoax. Then there was Nebraska Man. A single tooth was found and from that an artist for the *Illustrated London News* produced a picture of the ape-man and his mate which formed a double-page spread. The tooth was eventually found to be that of a rare type of pig — a herd of these pigs was even found some time later in Paraguay. It is not suggested that Nebraska Man was a deliberate hoax. But those involved were uncritical with the evidence because the atheistic evolutionist obviously expects to find evidence for evolution throughout nature.

Christ also said of the devil that 'He was a murderer from the beginning.'[8] This he became in the Garden of Eden, for Satan brought death to Adam and Eve. You remember the story: God had told Adam he would die if he ate the fruit of the tree of the knowledge of good and evil. 'Not so,' the devil contradicted. 'You will not die.' He implied that God was not being truthful, that it was safe to disobey God. Nothing unpleasant would happen. Down through the centuries, events have shown Satan to have been devastatingly wrong. Death entered the previously death-free world when Adam and Eve accepted Satan's lie.

The origin of the devil

God has not revealed Satan's biographical details. St John tells us that the devil sinned from the beginning.[9] As an angel created by God, Satan sinned by trying to make himself equal with God.

Does this make God the author of evil? Certainly not. All we know from Scripture about the character of God rebels against the very suggestion. If God created evil he becomes a fraud — worse, a sickening hypocrite, because he poses as loving and good, yet beneath it all he purposely created sin and death.

If the Creator God cannot be trusted, then *all* moral values would be suspect: *all* good, *all* love, would be in the realm of uncertainty. Man's worst nightmare — that all good is really evil, and love is really hatred — would become horribly true.

No, Satan was created good, but sinned of his own volition. He alone is the author of evil.

If God is all-powerful and hates evil, why does he not destroy Satan?

This is a long story, and we don't know all the details. But it seems that for reasons known only to God himself, he loves the human race, and it is his desire to call out a group of men and women who love him in return, not from compulsion, but in gratitude because he first loved them. In order to achieve this he introduced what we could call (in our human ignorance) an element of 'risk', whereby it would be possible for certain men and women, if they so wished, to reject his offer of love. Thus, the devil himself was permitted to sin, and to tempt into sin the first man and woman. Because they fell for his evil design, every human being subsequently has been a sinner; that is, our automatic inclination is always towards doing wrong, not right. So you are a sinner and I am too. In a strange way, therefore, Satan, sin and death are all necessary to God's eternal plan.

Can Satan do what he likes?

No! Satan is always under God's control. Nothing he does can be outside the permitted will of God.

Satan can go so far, but no further. If this idea upsets or even revolts you, answer this question. Which would you rather: that suffering came to you by blind fate, causelessly;[10] or that the devil was in total control and could wreak his hatred as he wanted, unrestrained; or that pain and suffering were permitted by a loving heavenly Father for your good, even though you cannot, at the time, see what the good is?[11]

In the long run it may well be that when in particular distress, all the Christian can say is, 'O God, I don't know why you are permitting me to suffer in this way, but I believe it must be for my ultimate good. I know that you are in control of the situation, and I trust you.' The atheist does not have this comfort.

12.
The Fall results in death

Adam and Eve had been told by God that they could eat fruit from any tree in the Garden of Eden, except fruit from the tree of the knowledge of good and evil. If they did eat that fruit, God said, they would 'surely die'. (The Hebrew literally means, 'dying, they would die', which makes it even more emphatic.)

Then in chapter 3 of Genesis we read of the serpent who spoke to Eve. As soon as he spoke, Eve should have known something was wrong. Animals don't talk. Eve must have known that. But this serpent did. She should have been alerted. The serpent asks a seemingly innocuous question: 'Did God really say that you shall not eat of every tree of the garden?' Only a little doubt. There is no harm in asking questions. I hope you have been asking them as you have read these pages. Eve replies, 'We may eat the fruit of the trees of the garden; but of the fruit of the tree which is in the midst of the garden, God has said, "You shall not eat it, nor shall you touch it, lest you die."' Eve is taken off guard. She does not seem to realize that she is talking to an enemy. She is also somewhat grudging in her reply. God had told the couple they could eat any of the fruit of the garden, with just one exception. Eve omits this. In the second part of her reply she adds, 'or touch it', which God had not said. Moreover, she leaves out that they would *surely* die.

It is not my intention to go through the chapter verse by verse. Read it yourself. The essential lesson is that eating the fruit of the tree of the knowledge of good and evil had been expressly forbidden by God under pain of death. Nevertheless, first Eve, then Adam, ate the fruit. I don't think we need assume there was anything poisonous or magical about the tree. (Incidentally we are *not* told it was an apple, in spite of what people commonly believe.)

In a way, eating the fruit was not the ultimate sin. It was merely the outward expression of disobedience. Disobedience (or rebellion) was the real sin. A direct, unequivocal command had been given — and broken. Such an apparently tiny fault, but what dire consequences for Adam, Eve and for all mankind!

Surely to take a bite of fruit is such a little thing? Yes, but as I stressed in an earlier chapter, the one who had commanded obedience was the Despot God, the awful Judge. There can be no trifling with him. His commands must be obeyed to the letter. I suppose the main difficulty we have in understanding this story is that, in our present age, absolute authority which demands instant obedience is virtually unknown. The green traffic light turns amber, but we drive on. It may be red by the time we clear the crossing — so what!

'Meet me at 2.30.' But 2.40 will do. 'No talking,' shouts the teacher. The hubbub slowly decreases to a low, persistent drone. In the twentieth century, absolutes of all kinds have been undermined.

But God's commandments are absolute and require total obedience. (By the way, if such an apparently minute infringement as eating a piece of fruit was condemned by God, what about the bigger things you and I do?)

Death

The first thing we have to understand about death is that it is not an inevitable pathological process. It is not *just* because the body is destroyed by accident, disease, or by wearing out. It *is* that, but only as the means by which death occurs. We learn about the *means* (which is shown on the death certificate) by reading textbooks of medicine, surgery and pathology. But the real, unseen reason why a person dies is because God in his sovereign will ordains that he or she dies at that particular time. Indeed, you can look at it the other way round: it is only because God *actively wills it* that we remain alive at all. In the Bible's book of Job we read,

> 'If [God] should set his heart on it,
> If he should gather to himself his spirit and his breath,

All flesh would perish together,
And man would return to the dust.'[1]

God is the sustainer of all life. If, therefore, we consider death in this biblical way, it is not strictly accurate to talk about physical, spiritual and eternal death as separate entities.

God is sovereign over animals as well as man. Jesus said, 'Not even a sparrow falls to the ground without your Father's will.' So it is no good to say, as some Christians who believe in evolution do, that the factor of death which entered the world because of sin concerns the human race only, and that therefore there could have been death for animals (including, of course, Adam's immediate forebears) before Adam sinned. No. The sovereign God is in complete control of all life and death, both of man and animals, including the lowly sparrow.

Death is separation

God told Adam and Eve that if they ate the fruit, they would die. Did they die? No, and yes. Certainly at the end of the day they were still alive and apparently healthy. In fact, we learn from Genesis chapter 5 that Adam died at the age of 930 years — a great age. *But he would not have died at all if he had not sinned.*

Yet something did happen immediately. Adam and Eve discovered they were naked. But they had been naked ever since they were created. We read at the end of Genesis chapter 2, 'They were both naked, the man and his wife, and were not ashamed.' Nothing had changed physically. They looked at themselves and each other and they were no different from what they had been the day before. Yet something *had* changed. Shame had crept in. Suddenly they felt the urgent need to hide their 'private parts' (note the term). The curtain of separation had descended, and the first evidence of this was shame. So they covered themselves with the only thing available, leaves. Then they heard the voice of the Lord walking through the garden in the cool of the day. And they hid themselves from him. They *said* it was because they were naked. But the real reason was because they knew they had been disobedient.

Disobedience to God (or call it by its other name — sin) had four immediate effects.

1. It cut them off from God

A barrier had descended between man and God. And that barrier resulted in spiritual death. Communion with God was lost from that time on. So Adam and Eve died spiritually from the moment they ate the fruit. And the first obvious consequence was that they tried to hide themselves. So, to answer the question, 'Did Adam and Eve die?' the answer is yes, spiritually at once, and physically almost 1,000 years later.

2. Psychological problems

Adam felt guilty. Otherwise why should he try to hide? Adam and Eve had suddenly developed a conscience, that little voice which whispers condemningly when we have done something wrong. As we saw in chapter 5, Freud taught that guilt is the primary psychological problem of the human race. And he would have been correct if he had meant true moral guilt in the eyes of a holy and righteous God (which he certainly did not). Only the story of the Garden of Eden tells us the origin of guilt.

3. Marital disharmony

The couple felt guilty when they looked at each other. That's why they used the leaves. Separation from God inevitably leads to separation of human beings, and is the reason for loneliness, divorce and murder. (We read of two murders in the fourth chapter of Genesis.)

God asked Adam what he had done. Adam passed the buck: 'The woman whom you gave to be with me [Your fault, God!], she gave me of the tree [Your fault, Eve!].' Eve passed the buck again: 'The serpent deceived me [Your fault, snake!].' Anyone who has done marriage counselling has heard such things before. But disharmony between husband and wife is but one example of the bickering and fighting so common between people. After all, if there is no higher power to whom to appeal, then men and women have to do the best they can with the light they have. We read this in the *Humanist Manifesto*: 'Humans are responsible for what they are or will become. No deity will save us; we must save ourselves.'

But what is to guide us as we search for good relationships with others? The good life for ourselves? The best we can do for the majority? But what about the minority? The best for the club, the political party, the nation? And behind it all is the belief that really man is an animal governed, as are all animals, by the laws of natural selection, survival of the fittest, and the need for food, sex and safety. Of course, if this is the world we favour, bickering and even wars are inevitable.

4. *Ecological separation*

At the end of Genesis chapter 3 we read that the earth grew thorns and thistles. Physical work, and the ability to perform it, had been one of the good gifts God had given man. But now sin separated him from the good earth. This may be a difficult idea to grasp, but Scripture teaches that *all* the evils of this world, including even ecological disasters, are the inevitable result of man's sin.

Listen to this passage from the Old Testament:

'The Lord brings a charge against the inhabitants of the land:

There is no truth or mercy
Or knowledge of God in the land.
By swearing and lying,
Killing and stealing and committing adultery,
They break all restraint,
With bloodshed after bloodshed.
Therefore [because of man's evil behaviour] the land will mourn;
And everyone who dwells there will waste away
With the beasts of the field
And the birds of the air;
Even the fish of the sea will be taken away.'[2]

Or listen to the New Testament: 'The creation was subjected to futility, not willingly, but because of him who subjected it in hope [that is God] … For we know that the whole creation groans and labours with birth pangs together until now.'[3]

Thus we see that ecological disasters are a direct result of the sin of the inhabitants of the land. Elsewhere we find that famine, earthquakes, floods and other natural disasters are also due to man's wickedness. The whole earth has been disrupted by the sin of man. In fact, all the pain and grief and horrors of life on this earth, all that is evil, is the result of man's sin. Evil and death entered the world as the result of the disobedience of one man, Adam.

But the New Testament passage quoted above tells us something else. First, we see that it was God who subjected the world to futility, purposely, by his own will. And second, that creation's distress can be likened to the pains of childbirth. Just as there is initial suffering but later joy when a child is born, so the whole of creation, though in futility now, can look forward with joyful anticipation to the redemption to come.

Why is everyone and everything involved?

You may ask, 'I can understand that if Adam sinned he deserved to be punished, but what has that got to do with the rest of mankind, the whole animate and inanimate world, and even with me?'

First, *Adam is the federal head of the human race.* He is the representative (one might almost say the spokesman) for all mankind. Adam's sin was not just a one-off problem, but carried permanent pollution with it — a pollution which, because of the solidarity of the human race, would affect not only Adam but all his descendants as well. As the result of the Fall the father of the race could pass on to all subsequent generations of mankind only a depraved human nature, polluting everyone and everything with which it comes in contact. Because Adam sinned, all men and women after him have sinned too.[4]

It is as though a genetic trait of sin has blighted every person living on the earth ever since.

Note an essential point: we do not *become* sinners because we sin; we sin because we *are* sinners — because we carry this trait, this innate tendency to disobey God. The disease is sin; the symptoms are sins. It is not because we commit some sins that we are sinners; it is because we are sinners that we are selfish, and all our relationships are soured.

Second, *death came into the world because Adam sinned.* Previously there had been no death — how could there have been? God, the man and woman, and the animals too, were in complete harmony with each other. There was nothing to mar their relationship.

But when sin entered the world, death inevitably followed, and for many people the fear of death is very real. Sin entered the world, and 'death through sin, and thus death spread to all men, because all sinned'.[5] Or again, 'The wages of sin is death';[6] that is, the inevitable consequence of sin is death — separation from God in this life, and eventual permanent separation from God in the life to come. Again, 'For since by man [Adam] came death ... by man came also the resurrection of the dead. For as in Adam all die, even so in Christ all shall be made alive.'[7]

But why should the whole creation be involved? Because, as the Bible makes clear, the whole world and all that is in it, indeed the whole universe, was made for the benefit and use of man. That is why the story of creation in Genesis 1 and 2 is so obviously given from the viewpoint of a human being standing on the earth, even when as yet no man had been made. We are told (for example in Psalm 8) that man is God's primary creation. Therefore, when man sinned he dragged down the whole material world around him.

Furthermore, since man has been given the oversight of the world as God's vicegerent, every error he makes, every evil he does, has its effect on the whole earth. History is full of accounts of corrupt rulers ruining the countries they have led. The former President Ferdinand Marcos of the Philippines is an example in recent years.

Of course, all this doctrine is utterly rejected by humanists. They would say it is ludicrous to think that man is the centre and most important feature of the universe. What utter conceit, they would say, for man is of no greater significance than a single grain of sand in the Sahara. Yet the Bible teaches that man is of such significance in the eyes of God that for him the Son of God had to come and die.

The Fall

The serpent episode is known theologically as the Fall. Man had previously been perfect, but he succumbed to the temptation of the evil one and sinned; thus he lost his close companionship with God.

If, as evolutionists believe, there had been no previous state of perfection, then there could have been no historical space-time Fall. Evolutionists maintain there was death before the first man (Adam) was born, and therefore before he sinned.

This is the crucial question: was there, or was there not, death on earth before Adam sinned? The Bible's answer is 'No'. Evolution says, 'Yes'. According to evolution there has always been death. Over millions of years, long before man, millions of creatures have died, including man's closest ancestors. In fact, if you believe the usual evolutionist story of Peking Man, some of man's forebears were cannibals. Death is an essential part of the evolutionary nature of things.

I have laboured this point because of the fundamental significance of death, both scientifically and theologically.

Scientifically, this marks the great divide between creation and evolution. Either over millions of years millions of creatures died, *or* no creatures died before Adam sinned. (Plants of course died. The Bible tell us that plants were given by God to man and animals as food to eat.[8])

Theologically, this will be the theme for the rest of the book. Suffice it to say that death is every bit as important for the creationist as the evolutionist but for totally different reasons.

13.
The law — historical

Perhaps in the chapter on the Fall I jumped the gun. After all, how can we know what God regards as obedience or disobedience anyway? What *is* right or wrong in his eyes? One of the girls who, with Charles Manson, murdered the pregnant actress Sharon Tate was asked by the judge at her trial, 'Don't you even have any remorse for what you did?' 'Remorse?' she replied. 'No, what I did was right for me.' I remember talking to a young man who told me, 'I've never done anything wrong,' and he was being absolutely honest with himself. His standard of reference did not include God. Therefore, according to his own lights he had never done anything morally wrong.

So the question is, how can we know what God regards as wrong, so that we can avoid it and not get into trouble? As before, we have to turn to the Bible for the answer.

The giving of the law

In the book of Exodus we read that for a period of about 200 years the children of Israel (the Jews) were brutally oppressed as slaves in Egypt. They had become a dispirited rabble, worshipping the nature gods of the Egyptians. Their morale was zero. But God intended to lead them out of slavery, through the desert, to the promised land of Palestine. By a series of remarkable miracles he freed them and brought them out. Their way was through the Red Sea, which, we are told, parted its waters to allow them to pass over on dry ground. The

Egyptians with their army and chariots tried to follow, but the waters returned and they were drowned.

Despite the many miraculous interventions by God on their behalf, the Israelites remained a rabble. In the wilderness, they grumbled against God and yearned for 'the fish which [they had eaten] freely in Egypt, the cucumbers, the melons, the leeks, the onions, and the garlic'[1] (how modern it all sounds!). Before God could make a great nation of them he had to instruct them as to what was right and what was wrong. So in due time he gave them the law at Mount Sinai. I have already referred to this event and to the terror the people experienced as they waited at the foot of the mountain for Moses to return. This law, given in detail by God to Moses, summarized as the Ten Commandments and enlarged and explained throughout the whole of Scripture, contains God's rules for holy living for Christians.

The law is contained in the Old Testament books of Genesis, Exodus, Leviticus, Numbers and Deuteronomy. Essentially it consists of three parts with some overlap. There is the judicial, the ceremonial and the moral law.

1. The judicial law

These laws were legislative and essentially practical. They were designed to instruct the Israelites in their behaviour under the harsh circumstances of the forty years of desert wanderings and their early establishment as a nation in Palestine.

The judicial laws were mainly concerned with aspects of public health. For me, as a medical practitioner, they are of particular interest. They govern such matters as the need to quarantine people with infectious diseases, the disposal of excreta and which animals are safe to eat.

To demonstrate their simple wisdom, let me set you an examination. *Question:* What general rules would you lay down for a crowd of perhaps half a million or more ex-slaves wandering in the desert to instruct them which animals are safe to eat and which are not? *Answer:* Those animals which have a cloven foot and chew the cud are good for food. So the pig, which has a cloven foot, might not be eaten since it does not also chew the cud. This was very wise as the pig is a notoriously dirty eater. The camel was also prohibited.

It chews its cud, but has large paddy feet for walking on soft sand. It was too valuable for transport to be killed for food. But, according to this regulation, the cow and sheep could be eaten.[2]

These laws are eminently sensible and appear highly practical even by modern medical standards 4,000 years later. Many foreshadow practices current today. And, in fact, their function is now achieved through our knowledge of bacteriology, biochemistry and other sciences.

2. The ceremonial law

Different ceremonies were prescribed for different circumstances. There were feasts and solemn assemblies for special occasions, for example, the purification of a woman after childbirth, and so on. Many of the ceremonial laws concerned sin offerings. An animal sacrifice was required if someone sinned against God's commandments. The person concerned had to bring the animal to the priest. The beast was usually a bull or a goat, sometimes a lamb, or, if the person was very poor, a young pigeon. The priest killed the animal and burned the meat on the altar. This was an offering to God to cleanse away sin.

Have you ever wondered why the practice of animal sacrifice is worldwide? From the ancient Greeks on the shores of the Mediterranean, to the Aztecs of Mexico, in the jungles of contemporary Africa or the highlands of New Guinea — all down the ages, a death has been required to placate the angry god. Strange, isn't it? The custom is so widespread. It almost looks as though the centrality of a sacrifice for sin has been implanted in the human heart from the dawn of time. The God of the Hebrews did not permit human sacrifices. But as the Israelites became exposed to the customs of the cruel pagans among whom they lived, they sometimes copied them, placing a squirming male infant on the white-hot metal arms of the heathen god Moloch.

The literal performance of the ceremonial laws was abandoned with the destruction of Herod's temple in Jerusalem in A.D.70. No longer was it possible for Jews, dispersed through the then-known world, to perform animal sacrifices at the stipulated location.

In practice, however, as we shall see, the God-ordained *necessity* for the ceremonial laws had already ceased with Christ's crucifixion. This was dramatically demonstrated by the fact that the veil in the Jewish temple in Jerusalem, which separated the outer courts from the Holy of Holies, was torn in half from the top to the bottom at the moment of Christ's death.[3] Why? Because it was no longer required.

3. The moral law

The laws which mainly concern us are the moral laws. They are found throughout both the Old and New Testaments, but the best-known version, which summarizes them all, is given in the Ten Commandments.

The Ten Commandments were given by God to Moses on Mount Sinai. They were written on two tablets of stone — 'written with the finger of God'.[4] The first tablet contained laws about man's relationship to God, and the second about his relationship to his fellow men and women.

The Commandments (found in Exodus 20) start off by telling us that God alone is to be worshipped. Then we come to the well-known commandment to keep the sabbath day holy. But the punitive 'don't-have-a-good-time-on-Sunday' attitude to sabbath-keeping is a caricature of what God intended. His concern was that people got adequate rest; personally I look forward to the weekends, don't you? But there is more to it than that. God said the sabbath was to be a sign between himself and the children of Israel for ever. For in creation, God worked on six days, and rested on the seventh. And so he commanded that we should do the same.

The second group of commandments deals with our duty to our parents and the people around us. You have probably heard some of these commandments before: you shall not murder, commit adultery, steal, lie, covet (to covet is to desire something which doesn't properly belong to you).

You mustn't think that by just keeping the Ten Commandments you will be all right. Have a look at them. You may be able to say that you have never bowed down to an idol (in the literal sense). Have you ever 'taken God's name in vain'? Well, 'Yes, perhaps,' you say. But not seriously. You may even not work on Sunday (the Christian equivalent to the sabbath). Very likely, too, you honour your father and mother.

You have not committed murder, etc. But even as I go through this list, I guess that very few people can really say in their heart that they have never broken a single commandment in their whole lives. But even this is not all. The Ten Commandments are only a summary of what God expects of us. Let me follow two of the commandments through so that you can see what I mean.

Murder

Take the commandment, 'You shall not murder,'[5] as an illustration. I am sure you can say confidently, 'Well at least I have kept that one.' But this is just an example or prototype of a whole family of sins. Actual murder is wrong — sure, but in the next chapter in Exodus (chapter 21) we find a logical progression: 'He who strikes a man so that he dies shall surely be put to death' (verse 12) is followed by, 'He who strikes his father or his mother shall surely be put to death' (verse 15) (even though the parents don't die) and, 'He who kidnaps a man and sells him ... shall surely be put to death' (verse 16). 'He who curses his father or his mother shall surely be put to death' (verse 17). So killing, kidnapping and striking, or even cursing father or mother, all equally carry the death penalty. The command, 'You shall not murder,' has been extended to include any violation of another person's body or even, in the case of the parents, their character. Other people are important. And Genesis 9:6 tells us why:

> 'Whoever sheds man's blood
> By man his blood shall be shed;
> For in the image of God
> He made man.'

Any violence to a person is wrong because man is made in the image of God. Man is not an 'it'; he is not an animal, not even a higher animal (*Homo sapiens*). Whoever he is, noble, poor, or of another race or colour, sodden with alcohol, mentally retarded, geriatric, a foetus, it doesn't matter in God's eyes, as all are made in the image of God. However marred by the Fall, the image (the hallmark) is still stamped on them.

But wait. In the New Testament Jesus extends this family of sins yet further. He quotes the commandment, 'You shall not murder,' but then extends it. 'But I say to you that whoever is angry with his brother without a cause shall be in danger of the judgement. And whoever says to his brother, "Raca!" shall be in danger of the council. But whoever says, "You fool!" shall be in danger of hell fire.'[6] So anger and the use of the terms 'Raca' and 'you fool' were all regarded by Jesus as extensions of the commandment not to murder. 'Raca' was a term of contempt designed to humiliate, denigrate, snub and undermine, the sort of expression heard on the radio during a debate in Parliament.

To call someone 'you fool' was the worst of all because here the object of the epithet is considered a non-person, valueless.

One last extension of the 'no murder' clause: Jesus told the Pharisees, who were attempting to kill him, that they had a family likeness to their father the devil for 'he was a murderer from the beginning ... He is a liar and the father of lies.'[7] The great lie of Satan at the 'beginning' was to tell Adam and Eve, 'You will not die.' By this he killed them. They died spiritually from the moment they believed what he said and ate the fruit.

So the command not to kill encompasses even spiritual killing. If I, or anyone else, tells you something about Christianity which is untrue, and you act upon it, then I shall be murdering you spiritually. What a responsibility! No wonder I am being so careful in what I write.

Adultery

Another commandment, not to commit adultery, can similarly be considered the index member of the species of sexual sins. Adultery in the strict sense of the word refers to sexual intercourse between married men and women outside of their own marriages, whereas fornication is intercourse between persons who are unmarried. But obviously the commandment is not limited to the former only. All forms of immorality are included: rape, homosexuality, etc. In fact Jesus went so far as to say, 'You have heard that it was said to those of old, "You shall not commit adultery." But I say to you that whoever looks at a woman to lust for her has already committed adultery with her in his heart.'[8] The Ten Commandments are certainly far-reaching. They encompass thoughts as well as actions. So I ask you, why do you read the juicy rape horror-stories in the local paper? Is it purely for sociological interest?

When we consider the moral law in detail, we find that God's laws, given in the Ten Commandments and throughout Scripture, are impossibly difficult to keep. So you may well ask, 'Then why did he give them?' That is a good question which I will return to later (see chapter 14).

Blessings and curses

At the end of the law is a list of blessings upon those who keep it, and terrible curses on those who do not.[9] Here is an example: 'If you do not carefully observe all the words of this law ... that you may fear this glorious and awesome name, THE LORD YOUR GOD, then the Lord will bring upon you ... extraordinary plagues — great and prolonged plagues — and serious and prolonged sicknesses ... Your life shall hang in doubt before you; you shall fear day and night ... In the morning you shall say, "Oh, that it were evening!" And at evening you shall say, "Oh, that it were morning!" because of the fear which terrifies your heart.'[10]

Conclusion

At the beginning of this chapter I asked the question: 'What is right and wrong in God's eyes?' Well, now you have the answer: a terrible list of dos and don'ts with curses for not keeping the law. St James makes it even harder, for he insists on the negative: 'To him who knows to do good and does not do it, to him it is sin.'[11] So it is not just a question of not doing what is wrong, but also of knowing what is right and then failing to do it.

People don't take much notice of God's law these days. I wonder why not. One reason is because we don't take the character of God seriously any more. No longer is he Creator and Judge. No longer has he the right to tell us what to do. No longer is he the Judge to enforce these laws. Much of Christianity has gone soft: 'God loves me and will forgive me even if I disobey him.'

I wonder how this chapter has affected you. Are you still prepared to say, 'I haven't done anything wrong'? Or is the whole matter too awful to contemplate, so that you will close the book and go and think of something more cheerful for a while?

There are two positive commandments which I want to leave with you.

Jesus Christ was asked which were the greatest commandments. He replied: '"You shall love the Lord your God with all your heart, with all your soul, and with all your mind," [that is totally, with no holds barred]. This is the first and great commandment. And the second is like it: "You shall love your neighbour as yourself."'[12] So the ultimate command is to love God and every human being. This is another command none of us has kept.

I hope this emphasis on love restores the balance somewhat. Yes, we have disobeyed God countless times. Yes, we deserve God's curse. Yes, we are doomed to die. Yet God has not left us without hope. The gulf between man's sin and God's purity may seem impassable. But God has devised a way ...

If you are really worried about what you have read, perhaps you should miss the next chapter and go on to chapter 15. But because I want to be logical and some people are still asking questions, I hope you will read chapter 14 first.

14.
The law demands perfection

The message from chapter 13 is profoundly depressing. God has given laws, but we each know perfectly well that we have no hope of keeping them. They are too stringent. Futhermore, if we only keep God's law outwardly, that is not enough. It is the inward motive that counts. Maybe I don't commit adultery. But suppose the reason why I don't is from fear of being found out. Or, perhaps worse still, from pride, so that I can say, quite accurately, but with stomach-churning hypocrisy, 'I wouldn't dream of doing such a thing.'

You see, it is possible to keep God's law outwardly, but reject it in your heart. And that is the worst sin of all. Jesus severely castigated hypocrites. Look at Matthew chapter 23, for example. There we read that seven times Jesus repeated, 'Woe to you, scribes and Pharisees, hypocrites.' He calls them 'serpents, [a] brood of vipers', and asks, 'How can you escape the condemnation of hell?'[1] And yet most of their contemporaries would have called the Pharisees the most highly religious, moral, patriotic men in the land. The law has to be kept in its entirety. To obey bits and ignore the rest is useless. If you don't keep the whole law all the time, from cradle to grave, you are under the curse of God — so the Bible says, and not in one place only, but all through.

Consider the Ten Commandments, plus the extensions to other parts of the Bible, as summarized by Jesus Christ in the Sermon on the Mount, and then expressed in terms of the negative by St James[2] — Well, what do you think? Surely not even the most hard-headed person can stifle his conscience, look God in the face, and say, 'I have never once broken any of your laws.' If this is all true, two questions demand an answer.

1. If God knew that no one would be able to keep his laws, why did he make them in the first place?
2. If they can't be kept, does it *really* matter after all? Perhaps I should forget all about them and have a party.

Why did God make laws which can't be kept?

This is a good question. Politically speaking, laws made but never kept are worse than useless; they are dangerous. They bring the whole judicial system into disrespect.

But what may be correct politically is not applicable here, because of the character of God. As I have reiterated, an all-powerful, all-righteous God can have nothing to do with evil of any sort. His standard is perfection. And this standard is demanded of his creatures too. Jesus said, 'Therefore you shall be perfect, just as your Father in heaven is perfect.'[3] But since we could never know what real perfection was, God made laws to show us. However, because God is just, he does not expect man to obey a law which has not been promulgated.

'Promulgate' is a legal term which means to publish by a public declaration. Let me give an example. Some years ago a small town in northern Australia installed its first set of traffic lights. Because the town is 500 miles from the nearest big city, many of the inhabitants had never seen traffic lights before. There was great excitement.

At last the lights were switched on. A few days later, early in the morning, when no traffic was about, an elderly man pedalled his bike slowly over the road junction. The lights were red. An officious policeman stopped him and explained that he had broken the law. The old man replied politely, 'Listen young man, I've cycled over that crossing every morning for the past fifty years. I always look up and down the street, and if there is nothing coming I cycle across. I'm not going to stop doing that, lights or no lights.' But he was wrong. What had been perfectly lawful for fifty years was now unlawful. The lights had been switched on. Do you see?

If God had not given the law, man could not have been accused of sinning. Paul puts it this way: 'I would not have known sin except through the law. For I would not have known covetousness unless the law had said, "You shall not covet."'[4] The lights had been switched on!

Guilt — again

So the first effect of the law is to accuse us. To quote Paul again, 'The law was our tutor to bring us to Christ.'[5] The law makes us feel guilty, and quite correctly so, because we *are* guilty before the holy and just God. Freud was right when he said that guilt (true moral guilt, that is) was the most important psychological disorder and that all mankind suffers from it. But he was wrong in his belief that it was because mankind had broken ancient, deep-seated sexual taboos. The reason we feel guilt (excluding, that is, the pathological guilt of a person suffering from psychosis) is because we have broken the laws of God. God has implanted a conscience in the mind of every person, so that even if we have never read or even heard of the Ten Commandments, still our conscience accuses us. We know there is an 'ought' which we should follow, and we feel uncomfortable if we do not do so. Here, as with the law of the land, ignorance of the law is not accepted as an excuse.

Why God gave the law

1. If God had not given us definite, unambiguous laws, we might have sinned against divine character without ever realizing it, and 'The soul who sins shall die'[6] whether we are aware of our sin or not. Furthermore, the Bible tells us that after death there is a judgement,[7] when we shall all be judged for the evil we have done in this life. If there were no way by which we could know whether what we had done was wrong, we could be justly angry if we were condemned. But we *do* know, because God has given us unmistakable laws and we and everyone else have failed to keep those laws. So really, God's laws show his mercy. He does not want to judge us unfairly. More than that, God does not want to have to punish us at all. He takes no pleasure in death, even that of the wicked.[8]
2. Another reason why God made laws is that, even though most people keep only little bits of them even that is better than anarchy. At least God's law indicates the way we should go. For example, if everyone obeyed the commandment, 'You shall not steal', and all its ramifications, such as not stealing one's employer's time by taking a long lunch-break, or not fiddling one's income tax return, then a smaller police force might be required, and some insurance

premiums could be reduced. So whether people recognize the moral law as being from God or not, it is valuable for society. Indeed, many laws in Western countries are founded on the commandments of God even though this is not acknowledged. English common law, for example, is largely founded on the Judeo-Christian ethic.

3. God gave moral laws for a third reason, but this will only be relevant if you are a Christian. To use the beautiful expression of the old Reformers, God gave laws as 'a rule of life to show the Christian how he should live in praise of grace'. This may not make sense to you yet. We will return to it later.

Before I go on to the question, 'If the law can't be kept, does it really matter?' I want to pick up a couple of points which may be worrying you.

Judgement

Jesus Christ said, 'The hour is coming in which all who are in the graves will hear his voice [that is, the voice of the Son of God, Jesus Christ himself] and come forth — those who have done good, to the resurrection of life, and those who have done evil, to the resurrection of condemnation ... I [that is, Jesus Christ, will] judge; and my judgement is righteous, because I do not seek my own will but the will of the Father, who sent me.'[9]

So physical death is not the end, whether you believe what I am saying or not. Indeed, whether you believe in God or not makes no difference. The highest authority possible, Jesus Christ the Son of God, states that there will be a resurrection for everyone. And you and I will be part of it. And after the resurrection comes the judgement.

You may say, 'What right has God to judge *me*? Particularly when it seems I shall be found guilty anyway. It's not fair.' Isn't it? If you say that, you still haven't come to grips with the character of God — his perfect majesty, his boundless purity. Who are we to question God's goodness or fairness? God is the umpire, and we have no right to question his rulings. You and I cannot hope to approach God with our sin-spotted lives. In the end, after life's curtain comes down, there must be a critique of the play, a judgement.

Pragmatically, I want a final judgement, don't you? A headline in this morning's newspaper reads, 'Tough time ahead in jail for paedophile chiefs.' The article continues, 'Two prominent members of the child sex group Paedophile Information Exchange who were jailed yesterday were told by the judge, "Yours will not be easy lives from now on." They had already been attacked in Old Bailey cells where hot tea had been poured over them while awaiting sentence.' They will have a rough time from other prisoners in jail. Yet some people who commit even worse crimes apparently get away with it in this life. Stalin died comfortably in bed. Doesn't your sense of justice demand that notorious evil-doers should be punished? Mine does. Fellow prisoners of the child sex molestation group obviously thought so too.

By the way, when you say something is 'not fair', where does your sense of justice come from anyway? Only from the Bible. Not from the idea of natural selection. Evolution does not know the concept of 'fairness'. It only understands violence, selfishness and cunning.

Punishment

If a person is found guilty of a crime, he or she is usually punished. Why?

Have you ever asked yourself, 'What's the point?' Frequently we read of prisoners let out of jail who repeat the same crime, or a similar one, straight away. So what was the point? I suggest there are at least three possible purposes for human punishment.

1. A person may be sent to prison for the protection of the community. A man robs a bank with violence. Bank cashiers demand that he be put away for a number of years for their own safety. He might do it again. They might get hurt next time.
2. As an opportunity to reform. This is based on the assumption that there is good in everyone, and that crimes are committed by those who are in some way disadvantaged. Their behaviour has been adversely determined by their heredity or environment. Events in the past, or in their physiological or psychological make-up, programmed them to behave in that way. They couldn't help it. They are victims of circumstances.

If this belief were totally true, the best management of the prisoner would be to place him in a reformatory, where he could receive appropriate education as well as psychological and social help. But such treatment usually fails because it ignores the basic doctrine of original sin. We do wrong not *primarily* because of poor social circumstances (although these may determine the type of crime we commit). We sin because we are sinners. We inherit the tendency to do wrong from our first ancestor, Adam. No education can alter that. What is required is not a new head full of bright ideas, but a new heart — a radical transformation of our total personality, what the Bible calls a new creation.

3. Some punishments are arbitrary, cruel or even designed to strike terror into the heart of a community so that no one will dare commit that particular crime again. This sort of punishment is seen, for example, in Moslem countries which practise public flogging or cutting off a hand for certain offences.

What about God's punishment for sin? God's absolute justice demands that the wrong-doer be punished for his actions. This is not for the purpose of reform, nor to protect the community, nor is it vindictive. The punishment prescribed is solely to vindicate and satisfy the absolute justice of the holy God.

Works

You may be thinking, 'Though I can't keep God's law fully, I will, I must, do my best. Surely God won't send me to hell if I do the best I can.' Again you have forgotten that God's standard is perfection; nothing less will do.

But suppose you do all you can. Will God overlook the rest? Let me give you a fanciful illustration.

You are being pursued by enemies. You come to a deep chasm with a surging torrent fifty metres below. What can you do? You search for a bridge. There is none. However, you notice a tree by the edge of the ravine, so you take out your axe and desperately hew away at the trunk. At last, with a mighty crash it falls in the right direction, and bridges the stream. You are saved. But as you climb nearly the whole way over the tree, you hear a splintering at the further end. The branches on the bank ahead are scarcely strong enough to bear the weight of the tree. Your added weight makes it collapse. A partial bridge is useless. Nothing but a perfect bridge fastened at both ends will get you over the chasm.

Let me give you another illustration. Some people think that God, through the death of his Son on the cross, builds a bridge which takes us almost over the chasm, but we have to add the end bit by our works. Together we build the bridge. But this won't do either. The Bible sums it up this way: 'All have sinned and fall short of the glory of God.'[10] It even goes further to say, 'All our *righteousnesses* are like filthy rags'[11] — that is, even the best things we do are not good enough in God's eyes. Because, of course, his standard is perfection, as I keep saying. And even if we do something good, our motive for doing it is never solely and absolutely to please God.

Perhaps you still think you haven't done much wrong. I used to talk to a man in a service station about this. We would sit in the back and discuss Christianity. From time to time he would go to serve another customer and return. It was a bit disjointed. He was happy to tell me had done nothing seriously wrong. He had a scheme. By his bed was a sheet of paper with a horizontal line on it. Each night when he went to bed he would mark on this paper the good and bad things he had done that day — good above the line, and bad below:

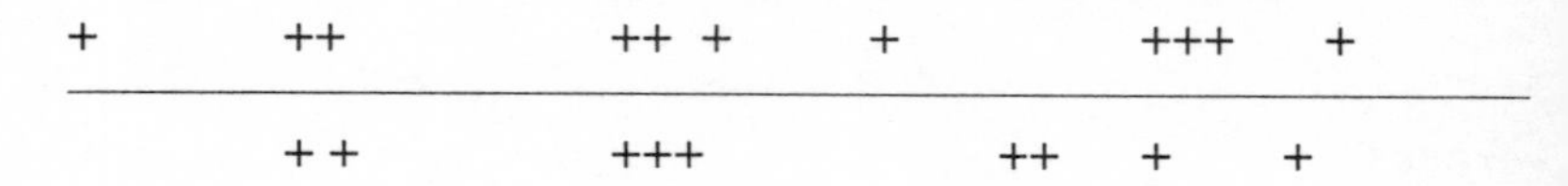

If, at the end of the week there were more crosses above the line than below, he was happy. But that is not the way God calculates things. His standard is perfection. No crosses are allowed below the line.

Does it really matter?

At the beginning of this chapter I asked two questions. The second was: if the law can't be kept, does it really matter? I'm sure by now you have guessed what my answer will be: yes, it matters vitally to you as an individual, more than anything else in life or death. I cannot stress the importance of this question strongly enough. Why? Let me refer you to the Bible again. St Paul writes (or rather, God the Holy Spirit writes through Paul), 'Those who do not obey the gospel of our Lord Jesus Christ ... shall be punished with everlasting destruction from the presence of the Lord and from the glory of his power, when he comes, in that day, to be glorified in his saints' (saints are believers).[12] This is what hell is about. Sin separates us from God.

If it were not that the Bible talks about hell — in fact, if Jesus Christ had not done so — I would certainly not have mentioned it. But you have to face facts. Hell is the place where God is not. It is a region where all beauty, all love, all peace and all happiness are absent. Or, to put it the other way round, it is a place of hatred, misery, guilt and despair. Every evil influence will be present in full measure.

To quote C. S. Lewis again, ultimately there are only two possible positions you can take. Either you say to God, 'Your will be done,' or God says to you, 'Your will be done.'

15. God's dilemma: two possible solutions

For reasons which we mortals can never understand, God desires the freely offered love and companionship of human beings. Why? I don't know. This profound mystery is hidden in the mind of God.

But if man consistently rebels against God, as he has done, what can God do about it? Let me state that last sentence again in more theological terms. Here is the dilemma: God is a righteous judge. All his actions are just and holy. He is also a God of love. He even loves those who disobey and spurn him. How can God reconcile these two aspects of his character — his love for sinner-man with his hatred of man's sin?

I am well aware that really it is not my place to ask such a question. Even to call it God's dilemma borders on impertinence, as though God were in some way taken by surprise by man's rejection of his love and he had, so to speak, to bring into operation his contingency plan. This is not so. The plan, as we have seen, was in operation from before the beginning of the world. Yet I ask again, faced with man's rebellion, what could God do? In his mercy he has given us some hints.

One way God could have dealt with the situation would have been to destroy sinful mankind, and start again with a new sinless race of man. And, in a way, this is what God once did.

The flood

After the Fall, described in Genesis chapter 3, the next chapters recount a constant theme of death and violence. Cain, Adam's eldest son, murdered his brother Abel. In the same chapter, we read of another murder by a man called Lamech. In Genesis 5 we have the recurrent statement: ' ... and he died ... and he died'.

In chapter 6 we are told that 'The Lord saw that the wickedness of man was great in the earth, and that every intent of the thoughts of his heart was only evil continually. And the Lord was sorry that he had made man ... So the Lord said, "I will destroy man whom I have created from the face of the earth, both man and beast ... for I am sorry that I have made them."'[1] Only Noah and his family were to be saved. God told Noah to built a great boat. Its dimensions are given. It was probably bigger than the liner *Queen Elizabeth*. Into this boat, or ark, Noah was to take his family, eight persons in all, and also a sample of all the animals. For God said, 'The end of all flesh has come before me, for the earth is filled with violence through them; and behold, I will destroy them with the earth.' But Noah and his family and the animals were to be safe in the ark.

Then God sent a great catastrophe which overwhelmed the whole earth. This is not the place to give a detailed report on the scientific and historical evidence for the flood. Many volumes have been written on the subject. Some are given in the bibliography at the end of the book. However a few facts are important in our present context.

The importance of Noah's flood in the creation story

You must realize that the creation model for the origin of life on earth is not complete without the story of the flood. Prior to the Fall there was no death, so all fossils must date from after the time when death came into the world as the result of sin. That is to say, all the animals of which we have fossil remains were contemporaneous with man. Probably the vast majority of the fossils we find today are the result of the catastrophe of Noah's flood. Almost all fossils occur in sedimentary rock, that is rock originally formed from sand, mud or debris laid down by water. The immense numbers of fossils all over the world, often occurring in fossil graveyards occupying many square kilometres, indicate a huge disaster. How else but by a massive flood could we get huge piles of dinosaur bones?

The only catastrophe of these dimensions mentioned in Scripture is the great flood of Noah. We are told, not only that it rained for forty days and forty nights, but also that 'The fountains of the great deep were broken up.'[2] There is no certainty what this means, but it could well mean that vast subterranean seas were shattered open by volcanic action. Some people believe that the cause of all this was that the earth was hit by a huge meteorite.

I have only said enough to show that historically and scientifically there is good evidence to believe in a worldwide flood. It is well described in the Old Testament, and there are frequent references to it in the New Testament as well.

The flood in God's providence

My purpose in alluding to the flood is this: God chose a good man (Noah), who was obedient to him, and from him purposed to form a new race. One might almost say that after the failure of Adam and Eve, God started again. But it didn't work. At the end of the chapter in which the covenant of the rainbow is described — when God promised he would never again send a universal flood to destroy the earth[3]— we read of Noah being drunk, and his son sinning because of it.[4] Sin is ingrained. It is part of man's very being. There never has been a sinless man or woman, apart from Jesus Christ alone. The scheme of wiping out the human race except for one good man and then starting afresh from him could never produce a new, pure, sinless human race.

Of course, I am not suggesting that God tried this method, only to find to his surprise that it failed. No, God knows the end from the beginning. The flood was a gigantic illustration of God's judgement on wickedness, and yet his mercy by not completely obliterating mankind.

And, incidentally, the flood provided the vast reserves of fossil fuels (coal and oil) so essential for man from the nineteenth century on. Yet, shame on us, today we take the sting out of the judgement story by making Noah's Ark a child's plaything.

The next catastrophe

Scripture not only treats the universal flood as a historical event, but also links it with a future event of even greater significance. St Peter tells us that just as 'the world that then existed perished' as a result of the flood, so too the present world we now live in is doomed, but next time the destruction will be by fire. Peter says, 'The day of the Lord will come as a thief in the night, in which the heavens will pass away with a great noise, and the elements will melt with fervent heat; both the earth and the works that are in it will be burned up.'[5] So, he asks, 'Since this is to happen, what sort of people should you be?'

The story of Noah's flood shows us that the virtual elimination of the human race did not obliterate man's sin.

How else could God have acted?

Forget the law and forgive?

You may say, 'Adam was called the son of God. If a son disobeys his human father, he may punish him, but then he forgives him.' I agree. And if the son disobeys again, what then? Further forgiveness with or without punishment? And again? Well, Jesus himself said that if someone sins against you, you should forgive him seventy times seven (that is 490) times.[6] And this really means for ever — infinity. Surely God does not demand a higher standard from us than he imposes on himself?

Yes, but — let me illustrate the problem by another story from the Bible. This story concerns the love which King David had for his son Absalom. Absalom was a man of violence and intrigue. He killed his half-brother Amnon because he had raped his sister.[7] So he had to flee the country. Some time later, Joab, David's general, arranged for his return from exile. Because Joab delayed in making an appointment for him to see the king, Absalom had Joab's field of barley set on fire. Nevertheless, out of love for his son, David agreed to forgive and reinstate him in the palace.

But Absalom repaid his father's love by scheming against him. He ingratiated himself with the ordinary people so that they would follow him. Then, when an opportunity presented itself, he ousted his father and placed himself on the throne. It was David's turn to flee. After some time, the rival armies, David's and Absalom's, grouped and the decisive battle was fought.

As General Joab was taking leave of the old king to go out to fight, David called to him, in such a way that all the people could hear, 'Deal gently for my sake with the young man Absalom.'[8] Despite everything, David's love for his son was undiminished.

So the battle was joined. Absalom and his army were defeated. As Absalom fled on a mule, he was carried under an oak tree. His long hair became entangled in the thick branches and the mule galloped on, leaving him hanging, trapped above the ground. There Joab found him and, without any compunction, thrust him through with a spear while he was still alive in the oak.

Two men ran from the battle to take the news to the old king. Ahimaaz arrived first. David asked him, with a catch in his voice, 'Is the young man, Absalom, safe?' To break the news as gently as he could, Ahimaaz replied, 'I saw a great tumult, but I did not know what it was about.' The second man, a Cushite, had no similar feelings. When asked the same question, he cried out pompously, 'May the enemies of my lord the king, and all that rise against you to do you harm, be as that young man is.' The king understood fully. His beloved son was dead. He was deeply moved and climbed slowly up the stairs to the chamber over the gate. And as he went, he wept saying, 'O my son Absalom — my son, my son Absalom — if only I had died in your place! O Absalom my son, my son!'[9]

But David was not able to die for his son. It would not have helped if he had. When Absalom offended he had been forgiven again and again. Because of his weakness, David had imperilled the kingdom. All David's army heard the king's request to Joab. They all knew what Joab had done. Instead of returning to the capital triumphantly as victors, they slunk home like a whipped cur.[10]

David the father loved his son and longed to forgive him yet again. But the ardent desire of David the father was not the correct action for David the king. He had already gone too far in forgiving and forgiving.

Have I explained the story adequately? David was absolute monarch and judge. If he forgave his son, how, in justice, could he sentence another person who came before him charged with the same crime? The country had already been driven close to anarchy.

God's dilemma is that despite his love, his holiness will not permit him to pardon us unless the penalty is paid in full. But the penalty is death.[11]

Summary

Let me underline some of the points in this chapter.

1. There is no good man on whom a new, perfect race can be founded. Noah and his family failed the test. He was a sinner like the rest of us.
2. It is not possible for God, the final arbiter of justice in the world, to forgive and forget sin as though it was of no importance. God is of purer eyes than to be able to look on evil.[12]

Sin must be punished, and the only punishment prescribed is death.

Yet God's dilemma remains. How can a God of love deal with man in his sinful state in such a way that God's own righteousness is not compromised?

Part 4

16.
God's dilemma: the supreme solution

David came close to God's solution when, in an agony of love, he cried out, 'If only I had died in your place! O Absalom my son, my son!'[1] David's death would not have availed, but his cry affords us a clue.

Go back to Adam. He was told that if he ate of the fruit, dying he would die[2] (Hebrew way of expressing emphasis by repetition). The penalty of disobedience to God must always be death, separation from God. Death is inevitable. This had been vividly demonstrated by the spiritual death of multitudes down the ages, and the physical death of all. 'The wages of sin is death.'[3] I cannot reiterate this more forcibly. And yet still God's love desires that men and women should not perish but should be reconciled to him.[4]

Animal sacrifice

In the Old Testament, God commanded that those who broke his law should sacrifice an animal. A bull or a goat died in place of the person. Blood was spilled, and blood is the symbol of life. Red blood coursing through arteries is the epitome of life, but when it flows from a body as a dull red/blue stain, it is the indicator of death — and always of a violent death.

The trouble with the Old Testament sacrifices was their impermanence. Suppose you do something wrong today; you sacrifice an animal.[5] But suppose you commit the same sin tomorrow; there will have to be another sacrifice. And so it goes on. You can never catch up. You can never keep the law adequately and know that God is fully satisfied. Never. We read in the New Testament, 'It is not possible that the blood of bulls and goats could take away sins.'[6] Yet these imperfect sacrifices pointed the way.

The law of God

So we are led to consider Jesus Christ, the Lamb of God, God's remedy for sin.[7] We have already seen him as Creator. He made us. He owns us.

Now read on.

1. Read in the Gospels how Jesus Christ, God himself, intruded into this world which he had made. God's plan, decreed before the foundation of the world, demanded the incarnation of Jesus to be fully man.[8] That is, he was to be integrally part of the human race, yet still God, and so in no way party to sin, and thus not subject to death unless he himself willingly agreed to it.
2. Read in the Gospels of the virgin birth of Jesus Christ, 'conceived of the Holy Spirit, born of the virgin Mary', as the Apostles' Creed puts it. Perhaps you say, 'Surely it is not really necessary to believe in the virgin birth? Many theologians reject it. No child has ever been conceived by a virgin.' But yes. The virgin birth, too, is an essential part of God's great plan. It is, of course, a creation miracle, of just the same order as the original creation. If you can believe the one, you need have no difficulty with the other. But, you say, 'The creation was x-thousands (millions?) of years ago.' As long ago as that, so we reason, anything might have happened. But Christ's birth was only 2,000 years ago, within the ambit of modern history. This is much harder to accept. And as I have explained before, the historicity of the Bible has to be accepted as a package deal. It stands or falls *in toto*. Believe the creation miracle and you can believe the lot. Reject the creation, and then, I agree, you are in difficulty with the virgin birth.

To return to the virgin birth: how else could God have shown that Jesus was at the same time both true God, and true man? You see, God's justice required that the same human nature which had sinned in Adam should make satisfaction to God for sin. Hence St Paul's insistence that 'Since by man came death, by man came also the resurrection of the dead. For as in Adam all die, even so in Christ all shall be made alive.'[9]

But further, this second Adam had himself to be sinless if he was to bear the sins of the world, and Jesus alone fulfilled that criterion. He is described by St Peter in pictorial language as 'a lamb without blemish and without spot'. Even his foes could not convict him of sin.[10]

3. Read in the Gospels of his amazing wisdom. Do you know the story of how the Jews tried to trip Jesus in argument? They asked him whether it was right for them, as Jews, to pay taxes to the hated Roman occupation forces.[11]

It was a catch-22 situation. If he had said 'No', they would have hailed him as a scab, a traitor. (Doubtless the Roman spies were listening too.) If he had said 'Yes', then he was no true child of Abraham. Would he incriminate himself? He was fixed. But no. 'Render ... to Caesar the things that are Caesar's, and to God the things that are God's,' Jesus replied. The Jews went away discomforted.

4. Read in the Gospels of his betrayal, his trial, his cruel death by the most terrible torture imaginable, crucifixion.

What is the meaning of all this? It is the story of God's solution. Jesus Christ, Son of God, Creator of the universe, God himself, of his free grace and mercy, loved you and me so much that he died on the cross *instead* of us, the just for the unjust, to bring us sinners to God.[12] For when the ransom[13] had been paid, the justice of the righteous God was satisfied. The judge had declared that a death has to occur before our sins can be removed.[14] And a death did occur — that of the spotless, sinless Son of God.

The curse

Look at God's plan another way. Earlier I told you of a long list of curses pronounced by God on anyone who did not keep his law in its entirety. Read the last of these curses, 'Cursed is the one who does not confirm *all* the words of this law.' St Paul puts the last curse this way: 'Cursed is everyone who does not continue in all things which are written in the book of the law, to do them.'[15] This means that everyone who does not completely obey the *total* law is under the curse of God. And that really does mean everyone.

But in Deuteronomy there is a particular and unexpected curse which I have not mentioned before, which tells us that a person who is hanged is 'accursed of God'. This is so important that the idea is taken up by St Paul in the New Testament. He says, 'Cursed is everyone who hangs on a tree.'[16]

Why was this particular method of execution singled out for cursing? It may have had local significance at the time Moses wrote. But its real importance did not surface until about 2,000 years later. For Jesus was crucified — hanged on a tree. And thus he bore the special curse of God. St Paul writes, 'Christ has redeemed us from the curse of the law, *having become a curse for us* (for it is written, "Cursed is everyone who hangs on a tree").' Jesus was cursed in order that you and I might be freed from God's curse for ever. No wonder that on the cross Jesus cried out in agony, 'My God, my God, why have you forsaken me?'[17] At that moment, as truly man, he was separated from God. The curse of God was upon him. He bore our sins in his body on the cross (or tree).[18] He who had never sinned became sin for us so that by his righteousness we might be made free.[19]

Sin and death for Christ — totally unwarranted; in order that there might be righteousness and life for us — also totally unwarranted.

The resurrection

Jesus died. He was buried. But he rose from the dead, and the resurrection is the seal of his sacrificial death.

If he had merely died it could have been a martyr's death only. Or he might have died for us as an updated animal-type sacrifice; far greater, of course, than the old Mosaic sacrifices, but still impermanent. But 'He was delivered up because of our offences, and was raised because of our justification.'[20] That is to say, he rose to make it 'just-as-if' we had never sinned. The resurrection is the seal to this. St Paul puts it as strongly as this: 'If Christ is not risen your faith is futile; you are still in your sins! ... For since by man came death, by man came also the resurrection of the dead. For as in Adam all die, even so in Christ all shall be made alive.'[21]

So we are alive. We have been given eternal, everlasting life.[22] True, our mortal bodies will die, but that is not the end. We will be raised with an immortal body, to live with Christ for ever. Death is defeated.

Another myth?

I know some people, even church people, will tell you the resurrection is just another myth. Perhaps, they say, Jesus never really died. He fainted on the cross, was taken down and recovered in the cool of the cave in which he was placed. But the Roman soldiers were experts. Their job was to make sure he was dead. Besides, a seriously injured man, left unresuscitated in a cold cave for many hours, does not walk out alive.

Maybe, someone says, Jesus never rose at all. But if so why did the Jews not produce the body? They had every reason for wanting to nip the resurrection story in the bud. They hated the fledgling Christian church, and if they could have produced the body, that would have been the end of it. In fact the Jews expected the resurrection. They had heard he would rise again. So they persuaded Pilate to allow them to seal the tomb and set a squad of soldiers to guard it. You can read about this in St Matthew's Gospel.[23] They feared the disciples would come and steal the body, then say he had risen.

Well, someone may say, maybe that is just what did occur. Yes, but only if the disciples were deliberate frauds. Not only did they deceive the Jews, but their friends, and even themselves. If the disciples stole the body, how do you account for the dramatic change in their behaviour after the resurrection? We read that at the time of the crucifixion they all 'forsook him and fled'. But afterwards they were bold to the extent of withstanding the Jews to the death. If you *know* your actions are founded on fraud, you don't behave like a lion. You definitely do not allow yourself to be killed defending a lie.

One last suggestion: some modern theologians reject the whole idea of a historical resurrection.[24] But St Paul takes great pains to refute the 'resurrection is a myth' notion. For him the resurrection was an indisputable fact of history. In 1 Corinthians 15:5-8 he lists some of the people who saw the risen Lord.

Here we come to the major difference between Christianity and all other religions. Christianity is based on space-time history: the creation, the temptation of Adam by Satan, the Fall, the virgin birth, the crucifixion and the resurrection are all historical, and to be believed as such. If any one of these is not 'true truth' (Francis Schaeffer's phrase) then there is grave doubt about all the rest.

Most importantly, Scripture links the historical fact of Adam's fall with Christ's resurrection. I have quoted this passage before, but it is so important that I must do so again. St Paul writes, 'If Christ is not risen, your faith is futile; you are still in your sins.' Further he links the historicity of Adam with that of Christ; 'For as in Adam all die, even so in Christ all shall be made alive.'[25] If there was no historical Adam, then there was no historical Christ. And, quite as important, if Christ really existed (and virtually no one denies this) then Adam must have been a real person too. As someone said at a Humanist Society meeting, 'Deny the absolute story of Adam and Eve, and you remove the necessity for Christ.' The humanist's theology was correct. If death did not enter the world by the sin of Adam and Eve, then the death of Jesus Christ on man's behalf was pointless. Christianity is a washout.

The resurrection is the key to Christianity

If there was no historical resurrection, then the creation story need not be believed; there is no reason to accept Jesus Christ as the Son of God; there is no hope of salvation for you and me. A man called Jesus may have died on a cross, but if he did not rise again it was just another martyr's death, and 'we are still in our sins'.

Lastly, if there was no historical resurrection, then there is no hope of a resurrection for us. We are, as Paul says, 'of all men most miserable', because we have been duped. Better never to believe in Christ at all, then to believe and find him a liar and the whole Christian doctrine a farce, and death a 'dead end'.

Is it fair?

I have been telling you that Jesus Christ died on the cross so that you will not have to die for your sins. You are pronounced guilty, but Jesus has taken your place instead of you.

Do you say, 'But that's not fair. One person can't take the

punishment for another.' In human terms, of course, that is so. David could not have died for Absalom. But there is a difference here.

Perhaps this illustration will help.

A king discovered that state secrets were being leaked to the enemy. He decreed that the traitor, when caught, was to receive forty-nine lashes. The traitor was found. She was the king's mother. What was the king to do? Justice demanded the full sentence. Love rebelled. The king tried the case himself, pronounced the Queen Mother guilty, then stepped from the throne, took off his crown and robes and told the executioner to administer the forty-nine lashes to himself, instead of to his mother. Love was fully satisfied.

But was this really justice? Why the special treatment? 'One law for royalty and another for peasants,' someone might say. The illustration is not fully satisfactory. No illustration ever can be. But Christ's death need not offend you. As I have tried to make clear, Jesus is not only Saviour, but also Creator. He made us. Therefore he has the absolute right to do anything he likes with us and for us. Of course love comes into it. He died because he loves us (just as the king took the punishment for his mother because he loved her). But further, Christ died for us because he owns us and he can do whatever he wishes with his own. He can extend his grace (that is, undeserved favour) or not as he desires. We, his creatures, have no right to question what he does. So it is not legitimate for us to say to the one who makes the rules, 'It's not fair.'

Of course I do not fully comprehend what God has done. This is the greatest mystery there can ever be. We finite creatures cannot expect to understand the loving mercy of the Infinite One. We have to accept it by faith and thank and worship the Saviour — or reject it all.

Summary

I started this chapter by looking at the animal sacrifices prescribed by God for the children of Israel. The problem with the Old Testament provision was that the sacrifices were impermanent. However, they served to point forward to the far greater sacrifice to come.

Then we considered Jesus Christ as Creator, the necessity for the virgin birth and Christ's perfect life, his death and resurrection — the central point in all history.

And so we come to the essence of the gospel story. Because we, you and I, are sinners, we are dead, alienated from God and therefore totally unable to do anything to help ourselves; we stand condemned, under the curse of the almighty Judge. But, although we read that the 'wages of sin is death', the verse continues, 'but the gift of God is eternal life in Christ Jesus our Lord.'[26] God offers eternal life to us as a free gift because Jesus Christ has died instead of us. This gift has to be accepted by each person individually by faith — and that is the topic of chapter 18.

17. Reasonable Christianity — summary so far

Earlier in this book I said that Christianity was reasonable in the broad, popular sense of the word. But reason can only get you so far in the search for truth. Reason is a matter of the mind, and our minds must be convinced that there are no flaws in what we accept. Difficulties, yes; even honest doubts; but no flaws. It is for this purpose that we have been given our minds, so that the Holy Spirit of truth can guide us into all truth.

As you grapple with accepting Christianity, emotions also play their part — fear, gratitude, love. Ultimately, however, Christianity has to be accepted by faith, as an act of the will.

Essential for Christianity, therefore, is a blend of the mind, the emotions and the will. And all must be accepted by faith.

Faith

What is faith? A schoolboy definition is, 'Believing what isn't true'! The mind must be the watchdog to see that this definition is incorrect.

What then is faith? A couplet answers this way:

> Faith steps out of the seeming void,
> And finds the rock beneath.

Let me illustrate. Some years ago my family and I were caravanning around Scotland. We had parked the van by a burn (a stream to the

English; a creek to Australians). In order to obtain food supplies, we had to cross the burn by stepping on stones. I had done this many times. One night the rain came down relentlessly. The burn became a torrent, hiding the stones. But we were running short of food. If someone had been watching, they would have been amazed to see me step out into the apparently deep, fast-flowing water. But I knew the stones were there even though they were invisible. 'Faith steps out … and finds the rock beneath.' As we shall see, reasonable Christianity has to be accepted by faith. The mind is vitally important, but it can only take you so far. Yet faith must be founded on knowledge, not a blind leap in the dark.

Simplistic

One problem with writing a book like this is that I have no idea who will read it. Obviously therefore, it has to be written so that it is understandable by the largest number of people. Some will have a far greater knowledge of science, philosophy, history and theology than I have. They may find this book simplistic. 'He just ignores the obvious difficulties,' they say. Let me answer in two ways. First I have provided a bibliography of books which have helped me to formulate my ideas. They may help you too.

Second, cut away the trappings of science, the smatterings of history, and the icing of philosophy, and come down to essential, biblical Christianity. And this we find is superbly simple. It can be understood by the dullest mind. Jesus Christ prayed, 'I thank you, Father, Lord of heaven and earth, because you have hidden these things [the mystery of the kingdom of heaven] from the wise and prudent and have revealed them to babes.'[1] Yet, at the same time, Christianity is so profound as to satisfy the greatest intellect.

Some people, on the other hand, may find the book not too simple, but too difficult to understand. If this is so, don't worry, grasp the essentials:

1. Man, God's special creation, was created good, without sin or death.
2. Man, tempted by Satan, fell into sin so that all subsequent men and women (including you and me) are sinners.
3. Sin cuts man off from God and causes untold misery and death.
4. God so desired the companionship of men that Jesus Christ, the

Son of God, the Creator, came to earth as a man, lived, died and rose again to pay the death penalty for man's sin once and for all.

5. But each individual has to accept this by faith. Nothing else you ever do is of so much lasting significance.

18.
The plan from the beginning of time

In this chapter I want to pick up the idea of God's total plan. But first we must pause. I have been using the words 'you' and 'we': 'we have eternal life'; 'we are saved'. But is this really so? Does this include you? Can you say this for yourself? The fact that Jesus died to take away the sins of the world does not necessarily mean that your sins are forgiven. It may have nothing to do with you. After all, there are millions of people who take no notice of the death and resurrection of Jesus. They may have heard about it, but have rejected it. Do they have their sins forgiven? Do they have eternal life? No. Salvation through Christ's death is freely available for everyone, but, sadly, not everyone avails themselves of it.

The Bible talks about being 'saved' from sin. Jesus Christ came to 'save' you from the inevitable punishment you deserve — death, spiritual and eternal. Whether you are a Christian or not, you will have to die physically one day. Death is the gateway between this mortal life and life hereafter, either with Christ for ever, or separated from Christ for ever, which is what the Bible calls hell, God, by his grace, has made this eternal life available to you. But the question is, do you want it? Jesus said that 'Whoever believes in [me] should not perish but have eternal life.'[1]

Eternal life

Before we go any further, think what becoming a Christian entails.

First *you have to acknowledge that you are a sinner, dead in your sins*. You can do absolutely nothing to save yourself. All your best deeds are like filthy rags'.[2] This hurts our pride. 'Surely,' you say, 'I have done *some* good things.' Yes certainly, in the eyes of men, and in your own eyes, but not before God. You see, he knows our hidden motives. He knows the real reason why we did those outwardly good acts. Remember the standard is perfection; nothing less will do.

Secondly, *you have to come to God just as you are: by faith*. 'By faith' means just like a little child who is asked if he would like some milk from the fridge. He holds out his hands and says, 'Yes, please.' He doesn't see the milk, but trusts you to give it to him. He knows you will not let him down. You have to come to Jesus as a little child and ask him to forgive your sins.

Jesus told a parable about two men who went into the temple to pray. One, a religious man, prayed like this: 'Thank you, God, that I am not like other people. I give money to good causes. I fast and pray. I am far better than that man over there.' The other man, well-known for his wicked behaviour, would not even look up. He hung his head and whispered, 'O God, be merciful to me a sinner.' Jesus said of the wicked man that he 'went away justified rather than the other'.[3] He had faith to believe God would be merciful and forgive him.

One gets the impression from the parable that the wicked man really was wicked. And this is important. No one is too bad to receive God's forgiveness. It doesn't depend on our 'goodness' or 'badness' at all. So however bad you think you are, and whatever awful crimes you may have committed, it makes no difference. Listen to what the Lord says: 'I will forgive their iniquity, and their sin I will remember no more.'[4]

Thirdly, *you have to realize that it is costly to be a Christian.* How costly it will be for you I do not know. I don't know your circumstances, What will people think of you? What about your friends? Can you take it? Think it through well before you act. You see, if you become a Christian it is not just that you accept a new philosophy. It is far more radical than that. You are re-created; you are given the mind of Christ.[5] You become a new person. Everything is changed: your desires, your ambitions, your emotions. In future it has to be Christ first and everything else afterwards.

You may well ask, 'But how can that happen? I can't live like that.' Certainly you can't. But God works a miracle. Just as he created you in the first place, so he will re-create you . Listen to these words: 'By grace [that is, by God's goodness and mercy, not because of anything you have done] you have been saved [from sin and death], through faith.' That is your part. You have to say 'Yes' to God. 'Yes, I believe. Please take away my sins and make me clean.' The verse goes on to say that even the faith we exercise is 'not of [ourselves]; it is the gift of God, not of works, lest any man should boast'.[6] Our salvation has to be by Christ alone, plus nothing.

From before the beginning

Scripture makes it plain that God has a plan from before the beginning of time.

In a sermon on the day the church was born (called the Day of Pentecost) St Peter said, 'Men of Israel, hear these words: Jesus of Nazareth, a man attested by God to you by miracles, wonders, and signs which God did through him in your midst, as you yourselves also know — him, being delivered by the determined counsel and foreknowledge of God, you have taken by lawless hands, have crucified, and put to death; whom God raised up, having loosed the pains of death, because it was not possible that he should be held by it.'[7]

Notice that, at the beginning. Peter reminds them that they all knew about Jesus. He had walked among them in Jerusalem and the country round about and performed miracles. He was one of them. Moreover, they knew well, and felt guilty for, the part they themselves had played in hounding him to death. It was their fault. Their lawless hands had done it. They were guilty. Yet, Peter says, Jesus had been delivered up by the carefully planned intention and foreknowledge of God. God has raised him to life again, because Jesus being God himself, the life-giver, death could not hold him.

So Christ's death for us was planned from eternity. If you become a Christian, that was planned too — in fact, from before the beginning of the world. Paul wrote, 'He [God] chose us in him before the foundation of the world, that we should be holy and without blame before him in love, having predestined us ...'[8] So although you believe by faith that Jesus Christ died to take away your sins, and that he will re-create you as a new person, and that one day you will go to live with Christ in glory — although all this is grasped and accepted by your mind through faith — yet it remains true that you had already been chosen to be a follower of Jesus from before the beginning, before the events of Genesis 1:1.

This is going to be difficult for you to grasp.

The Bible explains it this way. On one occasion St Paul had been preaching to the Jews, but they opposed him, contradicting and blaspheming. So Paul said, 'It was necessary that the word of God should be spoken to you first; but *since you reject it*, and judge yourselves unworthy of everlasting life, behold, we turn to the Gentiles.' The passage goes on: 'Now when the Gentiles heard this, they were glad and glorified the word of the Lord. And *as many as had been appointed to eternal life* believed.'[9] Do you see? The Jews had been offered the gospel but they had deliberately rejected it. They refused the offer of salvation through Jesus Christ, and the responsibility for doing so rested squarely on their shoulders. But the salvation of the Gentiles who believed was entirely from the Lord. It was God who had appointed them to eternal life. If you believe in Jesus Christ as your Saviour, this is because you are one of the 'elect', a chosen one. But if you reject God's appointed way to get right with him, you cannot blame God; it is entirely your own fault, and you will have to take the consequences, in this life and in the life to come, which for you will be hell.

The doctrine of God's 'choosing' or 'election' is important because it is God's guarantee. This order is this:

1. Being chosen by the will of God (predestination; election).
2. Hearing the gospel (the good news of salvation).
3. Believing by faith.
4. Being sealed by the Holy Spirit.[10]

Some gospel preachers leave out the part about predestination and election. But the danger then is that salvation becomes man-centred. It becomes a matter of, 'I have faith. I believe.'

It is only too possible to have faith in your own faith. People believe in the fact that they believe. But if this is all there is, how can I be certain that I am really a Christian? Suppose I stop believing tomorrow; perhaps my faith fails. Do I cease to be a Christian? No. The certainty of whether I am a Christian or not does not depend on me, but on God.

When I became a Christian someone told me a verse: 'If we

confess our sins, he [God] is faithful and just to forgive us our sins and to cleanse us from all unrighteousness.'[11] So my Christian faith does not depend on me but on God. And he is entirely trustworthy.

Unfortunately, however, I did not learn the lesson. After a few years I started to doubt whether I really was a Christian. I didn't feel or act like one. I forgot to pray and fell asleep reading the Bible. Then I would go and talk to some older Christian. Several times I was told, 'It doesn't matter about the past. Come to Jesus now. Believe on him now.' ('Just in case,' they almost said, 'just in case you didn't do it properly last time.') So I 'accepted Christ' again and again. It took many years to learn that whether I was a Christian or not did not depend on the strength of *my* faith, but on God's faithfulness. I had been 'chosen in Christ from before the foundation of the world'.

Let me allay a fear that you might have. Some people say, 'But what if I am not one of God's elect? Then there is no hope for me.' Don't fear. God has said, 'The one who comes to me [in faith] I will by no means cast out.'[12]

God does not want you to die. The message of the whole Bible proves that. Jesus said that 'God so loved the world that he gave his only begotten Son, that whoever believes in him should not perish but have everlasting life. For God did not send his Son into the world to condemn the world, but that the world through him might be saved.'[13] How can you tell if you are chosen? By coming to God by faith. Forget your doubts. Cry to him and you will find he will accept you, whoever you are, irrespective of how bad you are. No one is too bad for God to forgive. I can promise you that on the surety of the Word of God.

The plan

God's plan is that you should be able to say with complete confidence:

1. Christ created me.[14]
2. Christ has chosen me from before the beginning of the world.[15]
3. Christ has died for me.[16]
4. Christ has redeemed me from the curse.[17]
5. Christ has justified me[18](and made me 'just-as-if-I'd never sinned).
6. Christ has re-created me to be a new person.[19]

7. Christ, by his grace, has given me the faith to believe his promise.[20]
8. I am Christ's for ever because of what he has done.[21]
9. And all this has been sealed by the Holy Spirit.[22]

Notice what is Christ's part, your part and the Holy Spirit's part. This was the plan of God from the beginning, so it doesn't depend on your feelings. Once you have taken the step, it depends on God's faithfulness, and he won't let you down.

One last thing: if you have become a Christian, tell someone as soon as you can.[23] Find other Christians and link up with a Bible-believing church. Pray to God constantly. Thank him for all he has done for you. Bring your requests to him. Study the Bible; it is your instruction book from now on.

19.
The Christian life[1]

When you become a Christian the pin-ups on your wall won't shrivel up. The sexy blasphemous shows on your television will still be there if you care to switch the set on. The newspaper will still tell you about the latest violence. People on the bus won't look any happier. The men or women you work with will still expect you to go to bed with them. In fact, it will be the same old world as before.

Yet Jesus told his disciples (you too, if you are a Christian) that they would be *in* the world, but not *of* it.[2] That means, almost certainly, that God doesn't want you to leave your present job and go into a convent. You are to be a completely different person, but in your same environment.

However, although you remain *in* the world, you must not be *of* the world.

That is what St John says: 'Do not love the world or the things in the world. If anyone loves the world, the love of the Father is not in him. For all that is in the world — the lust of the flesh [lust = excessive desire], the lust of the eyes, and the pride of life — is not of the Father but is of the world. And the world is passing away, and the lust of it; but he who does the will of God abides for ever.'[3]

The law

What has happened to the law for the Christian? It's still there. But you are no longer under the law. You are under grace. You are free.

That means that because of Christ's death God has forgiven you your sins, past, present and future. Yes, future too. The penalty — death — which you deserved for not keeping the law has gone. Jesus Christ has taken it away. The veil of the old Jerusalem temple which screened the Holy of Holies has been torn down. The old Jewish ceremonial law is finished. No more animal sacrifices for sins are required. Christ has died. Christ has risen. If this were not so, you would still be trying to 'earn' your way into heaven by your own efforts, by keeping the law. But as we have seen, this is impossible. So you are under grace. By God's mercy your sins are forgiven; you are right with God for ever.

Does that mean that I need take no further notice of the law, that I can do as I like? A most emphatic *no*. Certainly *not*. God has stated in his commandments how he wants us to behave: to love him above all else and to love our neighbour (and that means everyone) as ourselves.[4] He has spelled it out in the Old and New Testaments. Now that he has redeemed you at the cost of Christ's blood, how could you ever go back to your old sinful life again? Can you voluntarily go against his will? Paul replies with an emphatic, 'Certainly not!'[5] I can imagine no more pernicious doctrine. Jesus said, 'If you love me, keep my commandments.[6] *The* evidence that you are a child of God is that you want to do what he says.

Having said this, we can freely admit that some of the Old Testament laws are obsolete: the Jewish ceremonial law (as we have seen) and also the hygienic laws in particular. But the moral laws all remain.

Does that sound a bit complicated? How, in practice, do I know what I may or may not do? Paul laid down principles to guide us. Let us look at some.

At the time when Paul lived, it was apparently possible in pagan cities like Corinth to buy meat which had been offered to idols, cheap — on special offer. (Perhaps with no refrigeration, it wasn't too fresh!) Some Christians said, 'This meat has come from an idol's temple. We mustn't eat it.' Others said, 'Idols don't exist. They are nothing: just a bit of carved wood and some paint on it. I'm free. I can eat the meat if I like.'[7]

How did Paul tackle this one? It was evidently a hot issue and he devotes a lot of space to it. It also serves as a useful practical illustration as to how we should behave. Here are Paul's conclusions:

1. Everything we do must be to the glory of God. This is fundamental.[8]
2. We must not give unnecessary offence to our 'neighbour'.[9] That means everyone but especially fellow-Christians.
3. We are told not to judge each other. On a certain contentious issue I may not agree with you, but I must not judge you if you genuinely believe you are doing God's will. Our judge is God. It is to him that we have to give account.[10]

In praise of grace

In a previous chapter I said that for the Christian, the law is now a rule of life to show him how to live 'in praise of grace'. Well, now do you understand what I meant by that? God, by his grace, has saved you. In order to thank him for what he has done, you want to serve him faithfully all the rest of your life. But how do you know what to do? You look at the commandments, and especially at the dos and don'ts in the New Testament. For example, look at Galatians 5:10-25. There you will learn what sort of actions will be to the glory of God and which will not.

Meditate on what Christ has done for you, and then serve him faithfully in love. St Paul writes, 'Let this mind be in you which was also in Christ Jesus, who, being in the form of God, did not consider it robbery to be equal with God, but made himself of no reputation, taking the form of a servant, and coming in the likeness of men. And being found in appearance as a man, he humbled himself and became obedient to the point of death, even the death of the cross. Therefore God also has highly exalted him and given him the name which is above every name, that at the name of Jesus every knee should bow.'[11] What a Saviour! What a Lord!

The world right way up

When Paul went to Thessalonica the Jews accused him of 'turning the world upside down'.[12] They were quite right (except that I would say he was turning it the right way up).

The point is that Christianity is radically different from all other beliefs. You are now a new man or woman. You have been re-created in the image of Christ (stupendous claim). Your basic belief system has been drastically changed, so your behaviour must change too.

Scripture says you should be 'temperate in all things'.[13] That means no overeating, no drunkenness, no sex outside of marriage, etc. And on the positive side you are told to be unselfish, helping other people. Your main desire should be to bring glory to God. You want to serve him in love and gratitude for all he has done for you. The Christian is never off duty throughout his whole life. The older you get, the more like Jesus you should become. What a tall order! It would be quite impossible if it were not that the Holy Spirit gives you the power to live as you ought.

Assurance

'If I am a Christian can I be sure I shall always be one?' Yes. If you have confessed your sins to God, and truly asked him for his forgiveness, and told him that you will serve him for ever, he will keep his part of the bargain. He has promised that. You were chosen in Christ Jesus to be his disciple from 'before the foundation of the world'. Read it again in Ephesians 1:4. Remember too, 'If we confess our sins, he is faithful and just to forgive us our sins and to cleanse us from all unrighteousness.'[14] That is the promise of the immutable God who can never break his word.

You may fail the Lord, but he will never fail you. You are his for all eternity.

Lastly

'Now that I'm a Christian does it mean that I will never sin again?' No, I'm afraid not. You will still be tempted by the devil. He may try more subtle, less obvious sins to trip you up, like hypocrisy and spiritual pride, rather than stealing or sex outside marriage.

Read Ephesians 4:17-33. Notice especially the key words in verse 30: 'Do not grieve the Holy Spirit of God.' Ask yourself, 'Why do I no longer want to sin?' (Use being angry as an example.) Is it because people will despise me for my lack of self-control? Is it because people will say, 'I thought he was a Christian, but just look at him'? These reasons are good enough. But there is another:

because I know it will grieve the dear Holy Spirit,[15] who has done so much for me. Let me explain: suppose a child breaks one of the school rules and is found out. He is punished. That hurts his pride and perhaps elsewhere too. However, he can cope with that and holds his head high. The real trouble comes when he has to tell his father and mother. He knows he won't get any further punishment, but he anticipates the look of sorrow in his father's eye. He will be grieved, terribly upset. The Christian desires desperately not to grieve the Holy Spirit. He wants to show the fruits of the Spirit.[16] He wants to be like Jesus.

When he does sin, he can still ask for, and know he will obtain, God's forgiveness. But he must strive not to sin again.

One day in heaven with Jesus Christ there will be no more separation and no more sin. The effects of the Fall will finally be abolished. The Christian ardently looks forward to the day when the Lord Jesus will come again to earth to take those who love him to be with him for ever.[17]

Death will finally have no more dominion over him. Maranatha — that is, 'Our Lord, come!'

Appendix I: selected Bible passages

Your understanding of Christianity depends somewhat on your knowledge of the Bible. If you have not read it much, it would be a formidable task to start at the beginning and try to read it through. All of it is important and none redundant, and for this reason I am reluctant to select certain passages for you to read. However, to help you I have done so. Please regard this selection as minimal.

Old Testament

Genesis 1-3. Chapters 1 and 2 tell us how God made the earth and placed man and woman on it. Chapter 3 tells us what happened when man was tempted by Satan and sinned. All the rest of the Bible explains what happened as a consequence, and what God did to restore man to himself.

Genesis 6-9. Noah and the flood:
geologically, the world's greatest catastrophe;
theologically, God's judgement on the world because of sin;
by God's grace, Noah and his family were saved in the ark.

Genesis 11-27. The story of Abraham: his call, the promise of descendants even when he was old, his faith.

Exodus 1-7. The call of Moses. His encounter with Pharaoh.

Exodus 12-13. The Passover; the exodus from Egypt.

Exodus 19-20. The Ten Commandments.

Exodus 32. The story of the golden calf.

Job 1 and 2. Job is the story of a good man who suffers. Why? Chapters 1 and 2 give us a peep into God's control over Satan.

Psalms. All of them are good. Here are some of my favourites: 1-8, 23, 24, 51-53, 73, 78.

Isaiah 40-45. This is just a small selection from one of the prophetic books. It shows God pleading with his chosen people even when they reject him. The prophecy concerning Cyrus, mentioned in chapter 45, was made about 175 years before Cyrus lived!

Daniel 1-6. The historical record of a great follower of God. Nebuchadnezzar is a king well known in secular writings.

New Testament

Read one of the Synoptic Gospels (Matthew, Mark or Luke—perhaps Matthew would be best), then the Gospel of John. This was probably written last, and contains more doctrine than the others.

Acts 1-19. The historical account of the foundation of the early church.

Ephesians. A very practical letter by St Paul.

1 John. A short book by the writer of the Gospel of the same name.

2 Peter. Important because of its prophecy of the end of the world.

1 Corinthians. Written to a church which was going astray. Read particularly chapters 13 and 15.

Romans. A difficult book, full of deep doctrine, but essential reading if you wish to progress in knowledge of the Christian faith.

Revelation. Another difficult book. Read 1-3; 20-22. This is a 'vision'. It tells of things that will happen 'hereafter'.

Appendix II: summary of key statements

This appendix collects together key statements made throughout the book and thus comprises a summary of the whole book.

	Page
Prologue	
It is for people with problems, big problems and little problems, that this book has been written.	16
Christianity has the answer to guilt.	16
A supernatural is necessary	
At time zero there can have been no matter or energy, not even space for the matter to explode into.	17
There must be another dimension, a realm of the supernatural.	18
The question is, does the supernatural choose to reveal itself to us?	19
An intelligence is necessary for the scientist	
Amino acids are merely the building blocks, not the building.	23
I am constantly amazed at the complexity and intricacy of function in the human body, made up of millions of living cells.	24
The required formula is not just Matter + Energy + Time = Life But Matter + Energy + Time + *Programme* (DNA) = Life	25

Page

Before the beginning

Christians believe in God the Father, Jesus Christ, the Son of God, and God the Holy Spirit—God in three persons. 59

Jesus Christ is the eternal Son of God. He was and is God, the Creator of the universe. 61

The character of God (2)

We are not cosmic drop-outs. God is there. He has spoken. 65

Jesus Christ, the Creator of the universe, had a relationship of love and communication with God the Father before the world was founded. 66

Man

Man is an enigma, a paradox. 69

Man and animals have some likenesses, but even more differences. 71

Man is vicegerent (ruler under God) of the world. 73

The problem of good and evil

There must be two supernatural agencies at work in the world: God and his angels, and the devil (Satan) and his demons. 78

The devil is a liar and the father of lies. 80

Satan was created good, but sinned of his own volition. He alone is the author of evil. 82

Satan is always under God's control. Nothing he does can be outside the permitted will of God. 82

The Fall results in death

In a way, eating the fruit was not the ultimate sin. It was merely the outward expression of disobedience. Disobedience (or rebellion) was the real sin. 85

Suddenly they felt the urgent need to hide their 'private parts' (note the term). The curtain of separation had descended. 86

Because Adam sinned, all men and women after him have sinned too. 89

This is the crucial question: was there, or was there not, death on earth before Adam sinned? 91

	Page
A death has to occur before our sins can be removed. And a death did occur — that of the spotless, sinless Son of God.	119
Jesus died. He was buried. But he rose from the dead, and the resurrection is the seal of his sacrificial death.	120
If there was no historical resurrection, then the creation story need not be believed; there is no reason to accept Jesus Christ as the Son of God; there is no hope of salvation for you and me.	122

Reasonable Christianity

Essential for Christianity, therefore, is a blend of the mind, the emotions and the will. And all must be accepted by faith.	125

The plan from the beginning of time

'We are saved.' But is this really so? Does this include you?	128
First you have to acknowledge that you are a sinner, dead in your sins.	128
Secondly, you have to come to God just as you are: by faith.	129
Thirdly, you have to realize that it is costly to be a Christian.	129
If you become a Christian, that was planned too — in fact, from before the beginning of the world.	130
If you have become a Christian, tell someone as soon as you can.	133

The Christian life

For the Christian, the law is now a rule of life to show him how to live 'in praise of grace'.	136
You have been re-created in the image of Christ (stupendous claim). Your basic belief system has been drastically changed, so your behaviour must change too.	136
You may fail the Lord, but he will never fail you. You are his for all eternity.	137
The Christian desires desperately not to grieve the Holy Spirit. He wants to show the fruits of the Spirit. He wants to be like Jesus.	138

Bibliography

Books written from a mainly non-Christian standpoint

Norman Macbeth, *Darwin Retried,* Gambit Press, Ipswich, Massachusetts, 1971.

'This brilliant treatise highlights the shortcomings and inconsistencies of the neo-Darwinian theory' (Arthur Koestler). Entertaining, easy to read.

Michael Denton, *Evolution: A Theory in Crisis* ('New developments in science are challenging orthodox Darwinism') , Burnett Books, London, 1985.

A careful indictment of Darwiniansim by a molecular biologist.

Allan Bloom, *The Closing of the American Mind,* ('How higher education has failed democracy and impoverished the souls of today's students.') Simon & Schuster, New York, 1987.

This book received rave reviews in the secular press. It explains why 'truth is relative' for today's student.

General

Josh McDowell, *Evidence that Demands a Verdict,* Campus Crusade for Christ, 1972, Vol. 1.

A well-researched and comprehensive reference book on Christian apologetics.

Francis A. Schaeffer, *Basic Bible Studies,* Hodder & Stoughton, London, 1973.

A series of studies containing such topics as, 'The God of the Bible, Man and God, Christ the Mediator, Salvation', etc. An excellent follow-up to *Reasonable Christianity.*

Francis A. Schaeffer, *The Great Evangelical Disaster,* Crossway Books, Westchester, Illinois, 1984.

Demonstrates the dangers to true Christianity of a departure from Scripture. An appendix: 'The marks of a Christian', is a classic.

Louis Berkhof, *Manual of Christian Doctrine,* Eerdmans Publishing, Grand Rapids, Michigan, 1933.

An excellent synopsis of theology.

Books on creation

E. J. Young, *In the Beginning* (*Genesis 1-3 and the Authority of the Bible*), Banner of Truth Trust, Edinburgh, 1988.

H. M. Morris, *The Genesis Record,* Baker Book House, Grand Rapids, Michigan, 1976.

A scientific and devotional commentary on the book of beginnings.

H. M. Morris & Gary E. Parker, *What is Creation Science?* Master Books, El Cájon, California, 1987.

A good synopsis.

John Rendle-Short, *F.I.G.S.: Foundations in Genesis Series,* Books 1-4, Foundations Publishing, Sunnybank, Queensland, 1989.

Biblical studies for personal or group use.

Sylvia Baker, *Bone of Contention*, Evangelical Press.

Historical

Ian T. Taylor, *In the Minds of Men, Darwin and the new world order*, T.F.E. Publishing, Toronto, 1987.
Good historical review of the creation/evolution controversy.

H. R. Rookmaaker, *Modern Art and the Death of a Culture,* IVP.
An illuminating book showing how modern art reflects a whole culture — a dying culture.

H. M. Morris, *The Long War Against God,* Baker Book House, Grand Rapids, Michigan, 1989.
A readable reference book showing that evolutionary theory is a battle against God.

Ken Ham, *The Lie Evolution,* Master Books, El Cájon, California.
Shows why biblical creation is so important for understanding the gospel, science and the culture of today.

Videos

Ken Ham, *The Genesis Solution,* Films for Christ, Arizona.
Explains how Christians must defend the account of creation.

John Rendle-Short, *Evolutionary Theory: Impact on Science, Society and Religion*, Foundations Publishing. Queensland.
Three illustrated lectures on one tape. Explains why civilization is in such a mess.

References

Introduction

1. *Pre-evangelism.* To understand pre-evangelism, compare the way St Paul preached to Jews and proselyte Gentiles at Thessalonica (Acts 17:1-4), who already knew the Old Testament, and the way he dealt with pagans at Lystra (Acts 14:11-18) and Athens (Acts 17:16-34).

To the Thessalonians, he used the Old Testament Scriptures as the known base. He told them their expected Messiah (or Christ) would not come as a warrior king, but as a suffering servant (cf. Isaiah 53), and explained that Jesus of Nazareth, who had died and risen again, was the Christ. Many believed.

In Lystra, Paul was met by the pantheistic priests of the Greek gods Zeus and Hermes. We could equate them today with followers of the New Age Movement or Eastern religions.

In Athens he contended with Stoic and Epicurean philosophers.

Stoics were serious academics. They believed in Fates: blind, impersonal, material forces who controlled nature by natural selection. They could be likened to modern-day humanists, or dedicated, left-wing Marxists.

Epicureans pursued pleasure in sex, money, drugs and Lady Luck. They were atheists with no belief in an after-life or a judgement. Their philosophy was 'Eat, drink, and be merry — for tomorrow we die.' Today their motto would be, 'She's all right, mate.'

Notice how Paul deals with these pagans in Lystra and Athens. First he shows them God as Creator. Only at the very end of his seminar on Mars Hill does he mention Jesus (Acts 17:31), and even then not by name. He told them, '[God] has appointed a day on which he will judge the world in righteousness by the man whom he has ordained. He has given assurance of this to all by raising him from the dead.' Paul had discovered that to discuss Jesus and the resurrection (17:18) was useless until he had first laid the foundation of God as Creator and preserver of the world and of all men. But observe that although some of the hearers believed, there was no mass turning to God (17:34). That perhaps came later. We are not told.

2. 1 Peter 3:14-15.

Prologue

1. Please note that I am not referring to pathological guilt. This condition is an illness, usually associated with an abnormal degree of depression or anxiety. The treatment is medical. Antidepressant drugs from a doctor may be required.

Chapter 1

1. John Gribbin, *Genesis,* Oxford University Press, 1982, p. 5.
2. Universe is derived from the Latin, *uni* (one), *versus* (to turn). Literally it means 'all taken together', or 'turned into one' — *Oxford English Dictionary.*

Chapter 2

1. In case you are worried as to where the maggots *do* come from — they come from eggs. Flies lay eggs in the putrefying meat and maggots hatch out after some weeks. If the meat is kept covered, this cannot occur.
2. Fred Hoyle and Chandra Wickramasinghe, *Evolution from Space*, Paladin, London, 1981, p.165.
3. I define theistic evolution as any method whereby God worked through the biologically understood mechanisms of evolution, utilizing the process of natural selection, to produce plant and animal life, and finally, man.

Chapter 3

1. In this chapter I have used extensively and quoted from Colin Brown's *Philosophy and the Christian Faith,* Inter-Varsity Press, 1973. See also Norman Macbeth, *Darwin Retried,* Gambit, 1971.
2. He considered this was what St Paul was talking about in his letter to the Romans in chapter 1, verse 20.
3. Michael Denton, *Evolution: A Theory in Crisis,* Adler and Adler, 1985, pp.328, 342.

Chapter 4

1. Charles Darwin, *The Descent of Man,* John Murray, 1901 edition, pp.241-2.
2. Stephen Jay Gould, *Ontogeny and Phylogeny,* Harvard University Press, 1977, pp.127-2.

Chapter 5

1. Please see note 1 of Prologue (above).

Chapter 6

1. Genesis 2:18.
2. Matthew 19:4-6; Ephesians 5:31.
3. Luke 3:38.
4. Luke 9:10-17.
5. Genesis 12:1-3; 17:1-8.
6. Exodus 20.
7. For example, Isaiah 7:14.

Chapter 7

1. *Holy*, see Isaiah 6:3; 1 Peter 1:15-16. *Righteous*, see Jeremiah 23:6; 1 John 2:1.
2. For example, Luke 2:29; Acts 4:24; 2 Timothy 2:21.
3. Genesis 1:16.
4. Genesis 1:3.
5. Romans 9:19-21.
6. Genesis 18:25.
7. See Exodus 19.
8. Exodus 19:12-16.

Chapter 8

1. Genesis 1:26: see also Isaiah 6:8.
2. e.g. Psalm 19:1; Isaiah 43:1; Acts 17:24; Matthew 11:25.
3. John 1:1,3 (Authorized Version).
4. Hebrews 1:2 (Authorized Version).
5. Colossians 1:16.
6. John 8:58.
7. Exodus 3:14.
8. See also Matthew 26:63-65; John 5:18; 19:7.
9. Matthew 5:1-7:29 (especially Matthew 5:39).
10. Luke 3:22.
11. Jesus accepted the title of God, see John 20:28. Jesus is revealed as man (condemned by Pilate) and as sovereign King in 1 Timothy 6:13-16.

Chapter 9

1. 2 Timothy 3:16.
2. Warfield quoted Cameron N. M. de S: *Evolution and the Authority of the Bible*, Paternoster Press, 1983, p.25.
3. Exodus 31:18.
4. John 8:46.
5. Unfortunately when modern man thinks of love, he thinks of sexual love. Ancient Greek (in which the New Testament was written) has three words for love: *eros*, from

which we get our word erotic (this word does not appear in the Bible); *phileo*, from which we derive English words such as filial and philanthropy (this is illustrated by the love between parent and child) and appears frequently in Scripture; and *agapeo,* a specific Bible word which speaks of the love of God for mankind and the love man should show for God and his fellows.

6. John 17:24.
7. John 17:5.
8. 1 John 4:16.
9. John 3:16.
10. Genesis 1:31.
11. The fact that we see death and struggle today is not disputed. The point I am making is that this could not have been the method by which a *good* God brought the world into existence. Later chapters take this issue further.
12. Hebrews 11:3.

Chapter 10

1. C. U. M. Smith, *The Brain: Toward an Understanding,* Faber and Faber, 1970, p.350.
2. The term 'Cartesian' is derived from the Latinized name of the French philosopher/mathematician René Descartes (1596-1650). Hence 'pertaining to Descartes, his philosophy or mathematical methods' (*Oxford English Dictionary*).
3. John Rendle-Short, *Man: Ape or Image. The Christian's Dilemma,* Master Books, 2nd ed., 1984.
4. See Exodus 31:18.
5. Arthur Koestler, *The Ghost in the Machine*, Picador, 1975, p.19.
6. Vicegerent: 'A person appointed by a ruler to act in his place or exercise certain of his administrative functions' (*Oxford English Dictionary*).
7. Psalm 8.

Chapter 11

1. Richard Dawkins, *The Selfish Gene,* Granada Publishing, 1978, p.2.
2. The biblical authors, and especially Jesus Christ, speak not only of the devil, but also of wicked angels with sense and intelligence who are called devils or demons. For simplicity, I will not here discuss them further. You will understand this chapter better if you first read Genesis chapter 3.
3. John 12:31; Ephesians 2:2.
4. Ephesians 6:12.
5. Revelation 12:9-10.
6. John 8:44 (New American Standard Version).
7. John Calvin, *Institutes of Christian Religion,* Eerdmans 1983, Book I, Chapter XIV, para. 15.
8. John 8:44.
9. 1 John 3:8.
10. In Greek mythology the Fates were three goddesses of destiny.

11. For some biblical examples of God's control of Satan, see Job 1 and 2; 2 Thesssalonians 2:9-11.

Chapter 12

1. Job 34:14-15. See also Deuteronomy 32:39; 1 Samuel 2:6; Luke 12:5.
2. Hosea 4:1-3.
3. Romans 8:20-22.
4. Romans 5:12.
5. Romans 5:12,14. This is known theologically as the doctrine of 'original sin'.
6. Romans 6:23.
7. 1 Corinthians 15:21-22.
8. Genesis 1:29-30.

Chapter 13

1. Numbers 11:5.
2. Leviticus 11:2-8.
3. Matthew 27:51; cf. Exodus 26:31.
4. Exodus 31:18.
5. Exodus 20:13.
6. Matthew 5:21-22.
7. John 8:44 (NASV).
8. Matthew 5:28.
9. Deuteronomy 27:15-26; 28:15-68.
10. Deuteronomy 28:58-59, 66, 67.
11. James 4:17.
12. Matthew 22:36-39.

Chapter 14

1. Matthew 23:33.
2. James 4:17.
3. Matthew 5:48.
4. Romans 7:7.
5. Galatians 3:24.
6. Ezekiel 18:4.
7. Hebrews 9:27.
8. Ezekiel 33:11.
9. John 5:28-30.
10. Romans 3:23.
11. Isaiah 64:6.
12. 2 Thessalonians 1:8-9.

Chapter 15

1. Genesis 6:5-7.
2. Genesis 7:11.
3. Genesis 9:9-17.
4. Genesis 9:21-27.
5. 2 Peter 3:6-10.
6. Matthew 18:21-22.
7. 2 Samuel 13.
8. 2 Samuel 18:5.
9. 2 Samuel 18:33.
10. 2 Samuel 19:3.
11. Romans 6:23.
12. Habakkuk 1:13.

Chapter 16

1. 2 Samuel 18:33.
2. Genesis 2:17.
3. Romans 6:23.
4. John 3:16.
5. e.g. see Leviticus 4-7.
6. Hebrews 10:4.
7. John 1:29.
8. John 17:3,8,18,21,23,25. Note also the words in verse 24: 'before the foundation of the world'.
9. 1 Corinthians 15:21-22.
10. 1 Peter 1:19; John 8:46.
11. Luke 20:22-25.
12. 1 Peter 3:18.
13. Matthew 20:28; 1 Timothy 2:4-6.
14. Hebrews 9:22.
15. Deuteronomy 27:26; Galatians 3:10.
16. Deuteronomy 21:23; Galatians 3:13.
17. Matthew 27:46.
18. 1 Peter 2:24.
19. Even more than Christ 'bearing our sins' as Peter tells us — as though that was not enough — we read in 2 Corinthians 5:21 that God 'made him [Jesus] who knew no sin to be sin for us, that we might become the righteousness of God in him.' That is, Christ identified so completely with our sin that he even became sin for us. Sin and death for Christ — totally undeserved; righteousness and life for me — totally undeserved.
20. Romans 4:25.
21. Read 1 Corinthians 15:13-22.
22. John 17:2-3.
23. Matthew 27:62-66.
24. Bishop John Robinson wrote, 'What was central … for all the early Christians

was the compelling conviction that Christ was alive in them. The empty tomb was simply the external sign of what they knew within. It spelt "resurrection" only to those who believed in him ... and it was clinched and expressed for them in what we call "the appearances". Exactly how physical or psychological these were, I don't think matters ... Sometimes it was a sudden, startling conviction of Jesus's presence, as tangible as flesh and blood. At other times it was a more gradual recognition of him behind other eyes and lips. But supremely for them, as for succeeding generations of Christians, it was in the act more familiarly associated with him that he made himself known — in the breaking and sharing of bread.'

For the bishop, Christ's resurrection recurs with every celebration of the Eucharist. John A. T. Robinson (Late Bishop of Woolwich) 1967, *But that I can't Believe,* Collins, p.39.

25. 1 Corinthians 15:17,22.
26. Romans 6:23.

Chapter 17

1. Matthew 11:25.

Chapter 18

1. John 3:16.
2. Isaiah 64:6.
3. Luke 18:10-14.
4. Jeremiah 31:34.
5. 2 Corinthians 5:17; 1 Corinthians 2:16.
6. Ephesians 2:8.
7. Acts 2:22-24.
8. Ephesians 1:4.
9. Acts 13:46,48 (emphasis added).
10. Ephesians 1:4, 9-13.
11. 1 John 1:9.
12. John 6:37.
13. John 3:16-17.
14. Colossians 1:16.
15. Ephesians 1:4.
16. Romans 5:6-8.
17. Galatians 3:13.
18. Romans 3:24.
19. 2 Corinthians 5:17 (creature in AV = creation).
20. Ephesians 2:8.
21. Romans 8:31-39.
22. Ephesians 1:13.
23. Luke 12:8-9; Romans 10:9-10.

Chapter 19

1. There is no point in your reading this chapter unless you are a Christian.
2. John 17:11,14.
3. 1 John 2:15-16.
4. Matthew 22:37-40.
5. Romans 6:1-2, 11-12.
6. John 14:15.
7. 1 Corinthians 8:1-13
8. 1 Corinthians 10:31.
9. 1 Corinthians 10:24,32.
10. Matthew 7:1-5, 21-23; Romans 14:10-12.
11. Philippians 2:5-8.
12. Acts 17:6.
13. 1 Corinthians 9:25.
14. 1 John 1:9-10.
15. Ephesians 4:30.
16. Galatians 5:22-23 (compare verses 18-21).
17. See such verses as John 14:1-3; Matthew 24:30-31; 2 Thessalonians 1:7-10; 2 Peter 3:9-13.

Index